£7-5

THE CUTTY SARK

By the Author of

The Cutty Sark

Last of a glorious era

by

Alan Villiers

With an Introduction by

H.R.H. The Duke of Edinburgh

Hodder and Stoughton

London   Sydney   Auckland   Toronto

*First published 1953. Seventh impression 1971. ISBN
0 340 10516 x. Printed in Great Britain for Hodder
and Stoughton Limited, St. Paul's House, Warwick
Lane, London EC4P 4AH by Lowe & Brydone (Printers)
Ltd, London*

CONTENTS

Brief Bibliography

THE LOG OF THE *Cutty Sark*, Basil Lubbock.   Brown, Son and
Ferguson, Glasgow.   New edition 1945.
This is comprehensive, thorough, and interesting through-
out—a first-class piece of work.

THE CHINA CLIPPERS, Basil Lubbock.   Brown, Son and Ferguson, Glasgow.   New edition 1946.
This book deals with all the famous clippers of the China
trade.   Like all Lubbock's work, it is the product of original
and comprehensive research.   These books are recommended
without reserve to the student of the sailing-ship.

THE RETURN OF THE *Cutty Sark*, C. Fox Smith.   Methuen & Co.,
London, 1924.
Out of print.   An interesting and well-written account of
the *Cutty Sark* up to the time of her restoration by Captain
Dowman.

THE *Cutty Sark*—THE LAST OF THE TEA CLIPPERS, Dr. C. Nepean
Longridge.   Percival Marshall, London, 1933.   2 Vols.
Out of print.   Comprehensive study of the ship especially
valuable to the model-maker.

THE TEA CLIPPERS, David R. MacGregor.   Percival Marshall,
London, 1952.
A first-class study of the subject, with many good plans and
illustrations.

THE COMPOSITE TEA CLIPPER *Cutty Sark*, by Captain G. C.
Steele, V.C., R.N.   Article in the MARINERS' MIRROR—the
journal of the Society for Nautical Research, July, 1939.

Various articles in the magazine SEA BREEZES, the seafaring
magazine published by Charles Birchall & Sons, 17, James
Street, Liverpool: and in the NAUTICAL MAGAZINE, published
by Brown, Son and Ferguson, Glasgow.

ILLUSTRATIONS

INTRODUCTION

By H.R.H. The Duke of Edinburgh

A GREAT deal has already been written about the *Cutty Sark*. Basil Lubbock's " Log of the *Cutty Sark* " gives a wonderful picture of the Tea Clippers in the last days of the great square-rigged ships trading across the world.

In this book Alan Villiers has written a comprehensive history of the famous and remarkable ship from the time of her building at Dumbarton right up to the present day. For the *Cutty Sark* is still afloat and sound, the last and greatest survivor of the lovely sailing-ships which brought credit and renown to the shipbuilders and seafaring men of these islands.

Quite recently the *Cutty Sark* Preservation Society was formed because it was felt that just as Nelson's *Victory* commemorates the men and ships of the old sailing Navy, so should Woodget's *Cutty Sark* be kept as a permanent memorial to the sailing merchantmen who were the backbone of British supremacy at sea for so many hundreds of years.

I can think of no better ending for the story of *Cutty Sark*.

Chapter One

THE CLIPPER SHIPS

THE blue water turned easily to white at the little ship's keen bow and, passing along her sides, merged in her wake like a running stream, without turbulence. The straight wake gleamed upon the Indian Ocean for miles. The trade wind hummed gently in the high rigging, and the beautifully symmetrical sails pressed lightly on their tacks and sheets and yards. The flying-fish skimming before the keen, high bow flew from the breaking water there as if they were unafraid, and fled briefly only to allow the lovely clipper undisputed way. Not a cloud flecked the high dome of the deep blue sky. Not a curling sea broke the line of the sharp horizon. Flying-fish weather !

> I'm a flying-fish sailor
> Just in from Hong Kong . . .

The little black ship speeding under her three pyramids of shapely sails was not bound from Hong Kong. She was a clipper in the China tea trade. The name on her bow and stern was a curious one— *Cutty Sark*. Cutty Sark ? Whatever on earth was that ? That was not the only unusual feature in this ship. The year was 1870. Already the Suez Canal was open, and the high funnels of the brig and barque-rigged steamers were belching smoke whenever the wind was not fair for them, from the Gulf of Suez to Shanghai. Far-sighted shipowners were already sinking their capital in powered vessels. A Scot named McGregor, a Liverpool man named Holt, a group of Scots and Londoners who had founded the great P. & O. Line were already established steamship owners, and their vessels were running on regular schedules to the markets of the East.

Yet the *Cutty Sark* was a new ship, and this was her maiden voyage. She was designed as a tea clipper and she was in some ways the ultimate expression of that wonderful ship-form, the deep-sea, square-rigged racer—a beautiful thoroughbred of a ship if ever there was one ; and yet doomed before her first voyage. The canal of Suez, the steady and increasing improvement in powered ships, the growing demand for Eastern products which was to make the small parcel-carrier an anachronism—these handicaps against her were powerful. Though nobody on board then was aware of it, the little full-rigged clipper was almost an anachronism already.

Yet how lovely she was ! How beautifully she went about her portion of the world's work ! She was a gesture of defiance at the encroaching power age. To bring her few truck-loads of new season's tea to the London market, she had to sail 16,000 miles out and 16,000 miles back again, crossing the Equator four times, storming the whole length of both Atlantics and crossing the Indian Ocean at its broadest twice,

rounding Good Hope—that ancient Cape of Storms
—eastwards and westwards, fighting her way north-
wards and then southwards again through the whole
breadth and the total length of the Java and China
Seas, keeping off reefs, surviving gales, keeping steerage
way in calms. Throughout this whole time her only
motive-power was the ocean wind. Her passage and
her very hope of survival lay in the skill of her master
and officers, and the strong, able arms of her seamen.
Her "engines" were a gentle tracery of masts and
yards and maze of rigging developed by seafaring man
since time began, in long, unbroken line. Her hull
sped with the grace of a swift young fish through the
great oceans, and its strength was the pride of the
craftsmen who built her. Grace and beauty flowed
with her across the seven seas, and the sea used her
gently when it could.

The sea used her gently, though she was to become
one of the hardest-driven little ships there ever were,
to race year after year around Cape Horn with its
wild and dreadful seas, for which she was not specially
designed. The China tea trade was aptly called a
flying-fish trade, and the bulk of the sailing was in
the good weather zones. It allowed ships to be comparatively lightly laden, for tea was not a heavy cargo.
It was perilous enough, in all conscience. Yet the
Cape Horn trade by comparison was like a permanent
winter off Iceland compared with a Mediterranean
summer cruise. The Cutty Sark was to carry little
tea. She was too late for that. For hers was to be
a hard and often harassed life, of tramping with coal

and scrap-iron cargoes, of storming towards Cape
Horn 6,000 miles from Sydney, crammed to bursting
with Australian wool, and the ice-cold spray and spume
flying over her to her trucks. She was to have her
share of racing ! Almost a quarter of a century of it,
in the hardest trade of all : and then, thirty years of
tramping, carrying anything that offered, under a
foreign flag, while the powered vessels took over the
trade routes of the world so thoroughly that the part
of the pioneer sailing-vessels was—for the moment—
all but forgotten.

But the *Cutty Sark* survived—through two world
wars, through dismastings, strandings, and all the
perils of the sea. She sailed throughout the first
World War and was in graver peril during the second.
Then she lay in the London River, and the bombs
came perilously near her.

It is a miracle that she should still survive, and
it is in great part a man-made miracle.

The *Cutty Sark*, a full-rigged ship of 963 tons gross,
was built at Dumbarton in Scotland to the order of
a well-known London sailing-ship owner, Captain
John Willis. Captain Willis was one of those old-
fashioned shipowners who had themselves been masters
in sail. His father had been an owner before him,
and he was well established. He went to sea and
rose to become master in order to learn his trade.
He was a shipowner of a type now extinct in Great
Britain, a *personal* shipowner.   It was not so much that
he owned his ships outright himself, and did not

nominally head some public company which really owned them. He was more than that. He looked after his ships in much the same manner that a racing man would look after his best horses. Yet he was more than that, too, for his ships lasted longer than horses did, and they would involve him in losses even heavier than race-horses could if he allowed them. John Willis owned many clipper ships, among them such famous vessels as the *Lammermuir* and *The Tweed*. He had been brought up in the China tea trade, and he was far from alone in his opinion that the clippers would hold their own there for a good many years to come, despite the Suez Canal and the increasing fleets of steamers. Steamships then were more often auxiliary sailing-vessels. Willis liked his ships real, without noisy engines in them and hordes of firemen, and a great propeller floundering away to spoil their sailing qualities.

Steam coal was expensive then, and steamships used prodigious quantities of it. An auxiliary steamer would take almost as long on the long voyage to Australia as a pure sailing-ship would, and it seemed then that the day when she could possibly carry bunkers enough to steam the whole way and somehow con-trive to fit a paying cargo in her hull as well, was in the unforeseeable future. As for Suez, it was enough for the old diehards that the ditch, as they called it, was French. It would probably cave in, or silt up ; or if it succeeded, be taken over by the Egyptians sooner or later, and made impossible to use. There was a real case for continuing to develop sailing-ships.

After all, it must be remembered that sailing-ships had been doing the world work then—all of its sea-borne trade—for a good many centuries. The ocean winds were reliable. There was an abundance of good sailing-ship sailors, though not of masters. Sailing-ships were still comparatively small and were not costly. Voyage costs were predictable. Owning principles were well established, and thoroughly understood. Defects in ships became immediately apparent, and could be dealt with. The trade in Eastern products had been, like every other trade, developed entirely by sailing-ships. It was the use of power in ships that seemed the anomaly then. " Bought wind," the old-timers called it, and asked, with good reason, why buy ocean winds ? Use them better—that was the answer.

It was to demonstrate, for her owner's profit and the good of the sailing-ship generally, just how best to make use of the ocean winds for the benefit of sea-borne trade, that old John Willis ordered the *Cutty Sark*. He was far from being alone in his optimism. The year she was built—1869, the year that the Suez Canal was completed—a dozen other lovely clippers were launched on both sides of the North Atlantic. Donald Mackay launched that lovely ship, the *Glory of the Seas*, and the famous *Great Admiral* also began her career that year. In the United Kingdom the *Caliph*, the *Normancourt*, *Ambassador*, *Duke of Abercorn*, *Oberon*, *Blackadder*, *Doune Castle*, and *City of Hankow* were among the clippers to begin their careers that year. The Australian emigrant trade was booming,

The clipper ship *Cutty Sark*, as she was in the wool trade from Australia.

As restored by Captain W. H. Dowman, and donated by Mrs. Dowman to become a tender to the training-ship *Worcester* in the Thames.

A famous clipper race—the *Ariel* and the *Taeping* in the Channel after racing from China.

The beautiful China tea clipper *Sir Lancelot*, from a contemporary lithograph.

and this was carried on almost exclusively under sail. The famous Loch Line was ordering its quartette of beauties, the *Lochs Ness, Tay, Katrine* and *Earn*. A good deal of the transatlantic passenger trade was still in the hands of sailing-ships, which had built it up to a state of remarkable efficiency. The Aberdeen White Star Line was building its first iron clipper, the *Patriarch*. The famed *Thermopylae* was a year old and had just made her wonderful maiden passage to Melbourne in sixty days. Sixty days to sail almost 15,000 miles! No steamship could hope to make a passage like that. Neither could any other sailing-ship, and none ever did again. But old John Willis cherished secret hopes that his *Cutty Sark* would sail the sticks out of the *Thermopylae*. London to Melbourne in sixty days? Why not fifty-five?

This was in the days before model experiments in tanks, or cold mathematical calculations, could compute the maximum speed a ship could do, before she was ever built. An owner backed his own fancy, and an owner who had been a clipper master himself and owned such ships as *The Tweed* with conspicuous success felt competent to dictate his ideas to designers and builders. When John Willis ordered the *Cutty Sark*, it was deliberately to lower the records held by the cock-sure *Thermopylae*—she already wore a gilded cock at her main truck—and to make such passages from China and from Australia as never had been made before.

In perfecting his ideas for the ship to beat all ships, John Willis drew heavily on the hull-shape of *The*

B

Tweed. This was a most unusual ship. She was one of the early vessels which had been built as a steamer —with paddles, not the hull-spoiling screw—and then, after a useful life, had the engines taken out of her and was made into a sailing-ship. She was built as a paddle-frigate for the Honourable East India Company, as the *Punjaub.* Shipowner Willis bought her and her sister-ship for £40,000, then promptly sold the sister for £42,000 and the engines and other junk out of the *Punjaub* for another £10,000. That is the sort of ship that owners liked in those days. Before she ever sailed to begin earning for him, the only capital he had in her was the sum he had spent on lengthening her and converting her into a cargo-carrier.

With such a beginning *The Tweed* could not go wrong. She was a powerful ship with a heavy stern and a look of massiveness and solidity. She looked more like a well-kept cart-horse than a race-horse to the connoisseurs, who liked their clippers graceful almost to the point of fragility. But the connoisseurs were wrong, for *The Tweed* proved herself a handsome racer right from the start. More than that, she was a money-maker. Like the four-masted full-rigger *Lancing* of later days—which also began life as a steamship, and did not look a particularly fast sailing-ship—*The Tweed* was in the class of the record-breakers. Above all, she paid handsome dividends.

Tradition has it that, before Hercules Linton was entrusted with the task of designing the new ship, John Willis took him to have a thorough look at *The Tweed.* Doubtless old " White Hat " (as he was

called because of the immaculate white topper he
always wore) expounded at length on the merits of
his favourite, and doubtless, too, the young designer
didn't really get a great deal out of the visit. *The
Tweed's* was a wonderful sailing hull, without a doubt,
but just why it had proved so sweet to move through
the sea with the sails spread from her combination
of masts and yards to drive it, no man could say.
She was something of a fluke, owing a little to the
lines of an old French Indian Ocean privateer and a
little more to the Asians who built her, and more
again to some happy circumstances in her lengthening. But how to reproduce these things ? That was
the problem. Hercules Linton was a first-class designer ; with or without *The Tweed* to help him, he
was going to produce a lovely ship.

One thing he did get from old White Hat's dis-
course, and maybe that visit to *The Tweed*, was the
idea of giving the *Cutty Sark* a more powerful stern
than other clippers had. Though the first requisite
of a clipper ship was speed, her hull was not meant
just to race through the water. It had to survive
in it, too. Many clippers were unduly fine. They
flung their sharp cut-waters into the seas and their
fine hulls followed through without, sometimes, both-
ering to rise at all, so that life aboard in bad weather
was like living on a half-tide rock. This could be
dangerous, especially in a heavy following sea. If the
great walls of water rushing at the running ship found
nothing aft to lift, then they were prone to break
right over her. It was dangerous for a sailing-ship

to take seas over her stern. Her poop was there, and her controls. Her controls were simple, for they consisted only of a hand-steering wheel, a binnacle to house the compass, and an officer of the watch. But they had to be safe. Watch officers were not to be washed overboard. Neither were helmsmen nor compasses. They could not be spared. In many clippers the helmsman was lashed to the wheel in bad weather, and the idea of that was two-fold. He had a better chance, probably, if a pooping sea broke over him ; and he could not lose his nerve and run away if a glance aft frightened him. As well it might !

But the *Cutty Sark's* helmsmen had to be lashed to the wheel often, too.

Hercules Linton was a partner in the young ship-building firm of Scott and Linton, and this was the firm old White Hat trusted to build his super-ship. Anxious for the business of so important a ship-owner, they cut things very fine. The contract price for the *Cutty Sark* was £21 a ton, and the specification was ruinous. Nothing but the best was to go in her—iron for her frames and the very best of timbers for her planking, and perfect teak for her decks. Every piece of timber, every fastening that went into her had to be perfect. Perfect timbers cost a deal of money, and a ship built of them cost more than £21 a ton, even in 1869.

The firm of Scott and Linton went out of business over the *Cutty Sark*, but not before Hercules Linton and his partner had produced the hull of a perfect ship. She was no copy of *The Tweed*, nor of any other ship. She was perfection in her own right. Others finished her when the young perfectionists could no longer pay their men. But she is their memorial. Her perfectly balanced lines and the magnificent Scots craftsmanship that went into her building made it certain that the *Cutty Sark* was no ordinary ship, even among the clippers.

No one could foresee that she would still be afloat when all her peers were gone and the very era that bred her seemed as remote as the Middle Ages, and even seafarers looked at her with astonished admiration, wondering that such vessels had ever kept the seas. She was fit to be a national monument, indeed. But how does it happen that she survives?

Chapter Two

IN THE CHINA TRADE

" CUTTY SARK " means, literally, short shirt, or short chemise, in the Scots dialect. It is taken from Burns' poem, " Tam O'Shanter," which had nothing to do with the sea except, perhaps, that its Rabelaisian quirks apply there as much as anywhere :

> Whene'r to drink you are inclined
> Or Cutty Sarks run in your mind
> Think : you may buy the joys ower dear,
> Remember Tam O'Shanter's mare.

Cutty sarks ran often enough in the minds of the old seafarers, but were not usually associated with hard-headed owners. It was an odd name. Whose cutty sark had old White Hat in mind ? Somebody's, that is sure enough. There was some real reason for choosing the unusual name for his crack clipper. No records remain that can throw light on the mystery now. Sailing-ships took their names from curious little things, in those days. Many of them had flowery names, like *Crest of the Wave, Herald of the Dawn, Spirit of the Morning, Lord of the Isles,* and so on. Many had a fine swing to them, or a challenge— *Fiery Cross, Flying Cloud, Sovereign of the Seas.* On both sides of the North Atlantic owners went in for

high-falutin names, or at any rate for those which
would look well on a sailing card. Just as the later
emigrant ships in the transatlantic trade went in for
large numbers of thin high funnels to impress the
peasants of Europe, the old sailors—and presumably
also the passengers going to Australia—loved names
like *Queen of the Colonies, Chariot of Fame, Dawn
of Hope,* and the like. Among such a rich collection
one would imagine that the short-shirted little witch
might seem a little odd. But the truth probably is
that the sailors of those days, and the waterfront
habitués who dealt with ships, took the name for
granted, just as they take the long Greek names of
the Blue Funnel motor-ships to-day. There was one
good thing about the name *Cutty Sark.* You could
at least pronounce it.

The figurehead was a special one, beautifully
carved for the ship by that past-master among carvers
of ships' figureheads, F. Hellyer of Blackwall. No
short shirt was allowed to show off the buxom lines
of the Scots' beauty. Her flowing garments merged
into the ship's cut-water as if she were a Greek god-
dess, and no man-chasing wanton. John Willis was
a bachelor, and he spared no expense either with the
carving of his witch or her companions. He had
Hellyer carve a galaxy of naked wantons dancing
along either bow, urging the lovely Nannie on with
her outstretched arm to pursue the fleeing Tam.
Tam himself, on his grey mare Meg, rode furiously
towards the scroll-work on the clipper's quarter. The
work was beautifully done, and one is left wondering

again what story lies behind old White Hat's choice of name and disregard of hard-earned funds to point whatever moral he might have intended. That carving was expensive. The naked witches were removed before the ship went into the Australian trade. They were too much of a good thing for the Sydneysiders.

The *Cutty Sark* was richly embellished in many ways. She was painted black, a jet and shining black, and her sheer was picked out by two lines of real gold-leaf. Gold-leaf adorned the letters of her name and her port of registry, London, and covered the laurel wreaths with which her counter was liberally decorated. Later in her career, she flew a short shirt in gilt at her main truck. The figurehead's outstretched arm was washed away in the down-south gales, and so was her head also, later on. Both were replaced, the arm several times, but not with the skill of a Hellyer.

It was with high hopes that the new ship was brought round to the London river towards the end of January, 1870, to load general cargo for Shanghai. Her master was Captain George Moodie, who had come to old Willis's favourable attention some years earlier as mate of *The Tweed*. Moodie had commanded two tea clippers—the *Laurel* and the *Lauderdale*. He was appointed to command the *Cutty Sark* shortly after the keel was laid, and it was the experienced eye of Captain Moodie that watched every piece of wood that went into the ship. He was a Scot, brought up as a fisherman and trained in the coastal and North

Sea trades. He was forty years old—a little old, perhaps, for a clipper master.

Driving clippers was an exacting life which threw an immense strain on body and mind. There were always more clippers than good clipper captains, but Moodie was a first-class man. He was a good reliable Scots' shipmaster, an able seaman and a good handler of men. He was a good business man too, and that was an important part of his qualifications, when the business success of a voyage was very much in the hands of the captain.

But Moodie had no luck with the *Cutty Sark*. Light winds and annoying petty accidents aloft dogged the little clipper almost the whole way to China. It was a running-in voyage, of course. In those days the making of iron-work to fit properly into the rigging of a deep-sea sailing-ship was not thoroughly understood, and a clipper's masts had to be stayed perfectly to do their work. Her standing rigging had to be set up with the fineness of the strings of an expensive violin, and it was by no means easy to achieve this perfection or, once achieved, to maintain it. Yet it had to be maintained for months on end, under all sorts of climatic conditions, and through great gales and long calms. New rigging was the devil, and it took time for all its parts properly to function. Moodie was a master of the art of rigging, but it took him most of the run from London to Shanghai to get the *Cutty* right. Meanwhile, her passage was spoiled. She did well, but she broke no records.

It was not the outward passage that mattered so much, though the masters did their best to make as good a run as possible. There were no premiums to be gained by bringing general cargoes to Shanghai more rapidly than other ships. It was new season's tea on the London market that made real racing worth-while. The *Thermopylae* had gone to Melbourne with a full hold of general cargo, and went on from Australia to Shanghai. The *Cutty Sark's* time from London was 104 days, and the old-timers— *Sir Lancelot* and *Taeping*—had little difficulty in bettering her passage. The *Lahloo* ran out in 98 days. The *Thermopylae*, on that run to Melbourne, was off the Cape only five weeks after leaving the English Channel. The *Cutty Sark* would obviously have to work hard to beat that handsome vessel—if she could do that at all.

The *Cutty Sark* was fortunate in getting a charter to load tea for the London market at a freight of £3 10s. for 50 cubic feet. Steamers had shown already that they could make the run to London in 60 days, despite the sailing-ship men's forecast that their firemen would all drop dead in the Red Sea. Liverpool owners and Liverpool firemen made the steamers a success, as much as anyone did. That remarkable specimen of humanity, the Liverpool Irishman, soon showed that he could stand up to the really devilish work of firing a coal-burner in the Red Sea, with a following wind, as easily as his mates stood the icy blizzards of Cape Horn. Liverpool Irish were strong, too, in the forecastles of square-rigged ships, and there were plenty of them from time to time in the *Cutty Sark*.

The Suez Canal showed no signs of silting up or caving in, and coal bunkering firms were doing very nicely at Aden and Colombo, and Singapore. Steamship competition was more than a menace. It was soon going to be fatal.

The new clipper loaded her first cargo of tea, and off she raced. She had no hope whatever of being first on the market, unless all the steamers blew up on the way home. But at least she could hope to be the first sailing-ship, and there were many in the trade who still believed that tea was contaminated by iron hulls and the fumes from stokeholds. Back in London, old White Hat was doing his best to foster this belief, which died hard.

The *Cutty Sark* was 110 days from Shanghai to London that first voyage. It was a good run, and better than most that season. But the *Thermopylae* was only 105 days from Foochow, and old Willis must have cursed. Owners and masters alike took a fierce personal interest in their ships and their passages, in those days. Captain Kemball of the *Thermopylae* was not as popular a figure in shipping circles as was Moodie, and neither was his wife who sailed with him. In fact there was no real comparison between the two passages. The *Thermopylae* sailed a month after the *Cutty Sark*. It was only when two ships could sail from the same port on the same tide that there could be a real match between them. White Hat bided his time, and went through

the logs with a large magnifying-glass. He could
find no fault in the seamanship recorded there, nor
did he expect to find any. Moodie had had to beat
the whole long and reef-strewn way down the China
Sea from Shanghai to Anjer. Once again, the new
clipper had more than her share of calms where the
trade winds should have been fresh.

This was especially the case in the Indian Ocean.
Moodie complained that he had no luck. Nonethe-
less he made the best passage of the group of clippers
which sailed about the same time, and White Hat,
though not elated, was still hopeful. The *Cutty Sark*
came storming up the channel in a south-west gale
and arrived in the Thames with many of her yards
fished where they had been over-strained by Moodie's
driving. She had time enough to lick her wounds
before setting out on her second China voyage. This
was in the spring of 1871.

Once again, the little full-rigger took general cargo
out while the *Thermopylae* went to Melbourne. Tea
clippers which took out cargoes to Australian ports
then went on to China through the Pacific, sometimes
with general cargo or coal, and sometimes in ballast.
Since they needed some ballast to go with the tea,
this was not necessarily a less profitable way of reach-
ing China than by going there direct. The *Cutty
Sark*, however, was in time to earn some money for
her owner by making a short run in the South China
Sea—down to Bangkok for rice which she delivered
to Hong Kong. She made this run while the new
season's tea was being prepared for the market.

When the tea was ready, however, the steamers took most of it. The previous year the steamers *Diomed*, *Agamemnon* and *Erl King* had taken tea to the London market in sixty days, via Suez, and though many old-timers sniffed at the stuff and swore that it smelled of anthracite or bilge water, or that it had obviously been roasted in the Red Sea, neither the trade nor the increasing number of tea-drinkers could detect anything really wrong with it. So there was a regular rush to build steamers. The clippers were offered only a miserable £3 for each 50 cubic feet of tea they loaded.

This would not do for the *Cutty Sark*. Though she was actually on the berth—and the *Thermopylae* was there with her, promising a great race—she was pulled off again by her agents, and sent down to Foochow. It was a foolish move. She couldn't even get an offer of £3 at Foochow and had to come sadly back to Shanghai again. This time she was lucky to get a cargo at all. Seven of the clippers loaded for New York where the new competition of the powered vessels was much weaker—they hadn't the bunkers to get across the Atlantic easily—but the *Cutty* had to eat humble pie and accept £3. She raced homewards with the famous *Ariel* and beat her by a week. It is fair to add that the *Ariel* was handled that voyage by a new commander who possibly did not get the best out of her. The *Thermopylae* had a better run than both of them, but once again the result was inconclusive. The *Thermopylae* had sensibly accepted what was offered and spared herself the waste of time in going to Foochow. Old Willis consoled himself

with the reflection that it was not the hated rival
which had the best passage. The little *Titania*
brought her tea into the London docks ninety-three
days after clearing from Foochow.

That freight of £3 for 50 cubic feet shook shipowner Willis, but did not deter him in his resolve
to stick to sail in general, and in particular to the
Cutty Sark. This freight was less than half of what
the clippers had been getting before the Canal was
opened. It cost a lot of money to keep a clipper in
good trim, and she could only pay her way if she
received good freights. She was essentially an express
and she had to be paid express rates. The most
serious thing was that the steamers could pay on lower
freights than the fine-lined clippers could, for they
loaded much larger parcels. It was all very well for
the clippers to pick up a few pounds by coasting
voyages, but there was not really much in these, and
the steamers were not handicapped by the sailer's
ability to make only one China voyage in a year.
The steamers could make two quite easily, and soon
they could make three, and even four. So they began
to take out all the general cargo, too. They had
another great advantage. They were *regular*. Shippers soon learned to appreciate that. After all, it was
a great help all round, in the business world, if any-
one concerned knew, almost exactly, when expected
cargoes were going to arrive. The clippers could
still race one another, but it became painfully obvious
to far-sighted merchants, owners, and masters alike
that it was a dying gesture.

But it took a long time for the diehards like Willis to admit defeat. He managed to get a general cargo for the *Cutty Sark* outwards to Shanghai again in '72, and delivered it in 108 days. He still had many friends among the shippers. The *Thermopylae* again went out to Melbourne and, in sticking to that trade, her owners showed good business sense. It was much more difficult for powered vessels to compete with square-rigged ships when the sailers had the advantage of the almost ideal conditions of the Australian voyage. To get to China they must work through the whole dangerous area of the South China Sea and, once they passed the barrier of the chain of Indonesian islands, the rest of the passage could be a nightmare. In that area the wind blew either from the south-west or the north-east, in alternating seasons called monsoons. If a shipmaster naturally preferred to wait for the monsoon which favoured him, the shippers did not. A monsoon in the face of an efficient steamer—and they were steadily becoming more efficient—did not bother her much, but it added weeks to a clipper's voyage. On the Australian run the sailer knew that she could " run her easting down "—storm along south of Forty S. from Tristan da Cunha to landfall off her Australian port—with an almost unbroken succession of westerly gales behind her. There were no bunker ports serving those wild waters. A steamer would have to stagger from Durban across to Fremantle, or from the Cape, which was further. If she sailed (as many did), then she stood to lose her advantage of predictable

arrival date.   If she steamed, she used so much coal
that she couldn't carry a paying cargo.

So there was still a future for square-rigged ships
at any rate in that trade, and the *Thermopylae's* owners
knew what they were doing.   There were freights
offering homewards from Australia in increasing
quantities, too, and the square-rigged ship—for the
time being—had an advantage over steam with these
also.   The shortening of the route to Australia by
using Suez Canal was more theoretical than real,
until steamers could be built more efficiently and
used less coal.

In 1872 the *Thermopylae* ran out to Melbourne in
sixty-seven days, which was a week longer than that
beautiful ship had taken on her maiden voyage.   It
was an excellent run, and when at last she was on the
loading berth together with the *Cutty Sark* in Shanghai
later that year, a good many knowledgeable shipmasters put their money on her to win.   At last there
was to be a real race—*the* clipper race of the century,
the last great tea race.   The ships were well matched.
The *Thermopylae* was a little the larger and had the
better record.   Her record was comparatively free of
the minor accidents which had marred the *Cutty
Sark's*.   She had been luckier with her winds, too—
and that was an important matter to a deep-sea sailing-
ship.   Her master, Captain Kemball, was well known
as a competent and fearless navigator as well as a
master driver of clippers.   He knew his ship well,
and he knew, too—better perhaps than Moodie did
—how to make the best use of all the divers channels

Captain George Moodie, first
master of the *Cutty Sark*.

Captain John Willis—"Old
White Hat"—built the
Cutty Sark to beat the
famous *Thermopylae*.

The Tweed was a converted steamer which sailed very well.
Ideas from her were embodied in the *Cutty Sark*.

The *Thermopylae* still holds the sailing records in the
Australian trade.

The *Cutty Sark* rigged as a barquentine during the first
World War, because of a shortage of spars.

and the changing conditions down the long and trying South China Sea. He had first-class officers and a good crew, well accustomed to the ship. From Kemball down to the cook's boy they all were determined to win.

The *Cutty Sark* was well-manned, too, and everybody aboard her was equally determined and confident. They had easily defeated the famous *Sir Lancelot* on the outwards passage. They swore, indeed, that they had never seen the ship they could not sail past. That was an old sailors' boast which was heard more often than it was substantiated. But in the *Cutty Sark's* case there was a good deal of truth in it.

The two ships dropped out of the Chinese port on the same tide and were promptly held up for three days in heavy fog. This was a poor way to begin a race which should have been so stirring. It was to have a poorer end. After a first-class sailing match all down the China Sea with now the one ship leading, now the other, the *Cutty Sark* had the great misfortune to lose her rudder in a savage gale in the Indian Ocean. She might as well have been dismasted. The *Thermopylae* suffered no such accident and raced onwards to come in an easy first, of course. But Captain Moodie and his men, far from being deterred by so serious an accident—for the ship was quite helpless without her rudder—set to at once and made her a new rudder, fitted it at sea, and sailed on. Again the makeshift rudder was carried away, and again they fitted another, and they put up such a

c

splendid performance bringing the deeply-laden clipper over 8,000 miles in her semi-crippled and hopelessly handicapped condition that the whole shipping world awarded the *Cutty Sark* the moral victory.

Moodie's seamanship, indeed, had been magnificent. Think of it! There was the ship, less than a thousand tons, jumping and leaping in the confused and dangerous sea left by three days of continuous gale. Always a wet ship, now she was almost as much under water as above it. The gale had been a very heavy one even for those down-south latitudes, and had blown out some sails which were sewn to stand up to hurricanes. However, she was holding her own and, indeed, doing quite well, until a tremendous sea broke under her counter and wrenched the wooden rudder from its pintles. The ship which had been rolling and plunging enough before, now began to roll as if she was falling right over. She fell into the trough of the sea, and the great combers creamed aboard her and smashed along her main deck. It was just as well that she was not opposing them or they would have smashed her. It was all very well to lie hove-to under a few rags of storm canvas, but somehow the ship had to be brought under control again, and that as quickly as possible.

There were not even any planks stout enough to make a temporary rudder from. Captain Moodie at first tried a spare spar out astern like a big sweep, but this was no use to the thoroughbred. He had to make her a real rudder somehow. Undeterred either by his wretched ill-luck, the gale, or the obvious handicaps of trying to carry out a major dry-docking job in the open sea with a deeply-laden ship which was trying to roll under, Moodie had all hands turned to. First they made heavy planks by sawing them bodily out of some spare spars—all clippers carried plenty of spare spars, for they knew that they might need them—and at the same time contrived the necessary ironwork to replace the lost pintles. The little ship had one good break. She had two stow-aways aboard who turned out to be excellent crafts-men, one a shipwright and the other a blacksmith. These two worked splendidly, and this must be one of those extremely rare instances when stowaways turned out to be of use to the vessel they were stealing passage in.

There was another person aboard who was no help at all; this was old White Hat's brother, Robert Willis, who was making the voyage for the good of his health. (He must have been a very healthy man to embark upon it.) When the rudder was carried away, Robert Willis cursed and raved about the poop like a madman, clamouring at poor Moodie to make for the nearest port. This must have been a trial, and Moodie promptly swore back at him and told him to go to hell. Robert Willis remained a sullen and useless critic throughout the proceedings and the rest of the passage, and the incident so rankled on Captain Moodie that he resigned his command as soon as he got home.

Despite the useless protests of the loud-mouthed passenger and all the other disabilities, a temporary rudder was made and properly secured, and the *Cutty Sark* was brought under control again. Still the gales continued to howl at her, almost as though old Neptune objected to her name, or resented the removal of the naked witches from the scroll-work at her bow, or for some other reason was determined to obstruct her progress. The new rudder was man-handled by a system of wires and chains leading to a spar across the poop and thence to the wheel, and she steered quite well. But the fresh onset of a row of gales on end put too great a strain on the jury rudder, and it had to be hauled inboard again for repairs. A second time it was shipped, successfully.

Fitting a jury rudder to the inaccessible stern-post while the ship was under way and leaping all over the place like a frisky two-year-old at a reluctant barrier, was a prodigious job. Everything was difficult, almost unbelievably so. Seas washing aboard continually upset the blacksmith's forge, which was a primitive arrangement at the best. One sea knocked down not only the forge, but also the blacksmith and the apprentice—Moodie's son—who was helping him. The forge full of hot coals fell on young Moodie's chest and the blacksmith was swept about the decks in the huge sea, still clinging to the bar of red-hot iron he had been working on. But he did not let go. Young Moodie, sworn at for wasting the fire, carried the scars of those burns all his life, and the blacksmith had his beard singed by the bar of iron. But they got on with the job again as soon as they could. The rudder was shipped, though on the

Sandridge Pier, Port Melbourne, 1874, with clippers loading wool.

The *Cutty Sark* waiting in Sydney Harbour for new season's wool, Captain Woodget in command.

second occasion this was only possible by slipping it
over the stern and then backing the ship on to it with
sternway, and reeving the rudder-post up through
the place for it.

Men who took this sort of thing in their stride
deserved to win. But the *Thermopylae* had stormed
along hundreds of miles ahead, and when she arrived
an easy first in the Channel, Kemball was cocky
about it. Of course, he did not know of his rival's
accident. He knew only that he had last seen her a
few miles away off Anjer and had heard nothing of
her since. When a few days later the *Cutty Sark*
came limping gamely up the Channel, racing under
a cloud of sail right to the last, even Kemball stared
when he heard she had come from the wrong side of
Good Hope with no proper steering-gear.

But he still declared that he had won. The argument waxed pretty hot, for the *Cutty Sark* was a
London ship and the excellent show she had put up
—it is doubtful if a handicapped sailing-ship ever
sailed from Good Hope to the Channel faster, and,
indeed, not many in perfect shape could show a
better passage—made her many friends. The English
love of the game loser made a real heroine out of
her, and before long it was Kemball who was being
commiserated. He refused point-blank to produce
the *Thermopylae's* log in order that it could be proved
which ship was ahead up to the time the *Cutty Sark*
lost her rudder—there is little doubt that the Londoner
was ahead then—and that piece of poor sportsmanship
lost him many supporters.

But Captain Moodie had had enough. He left the *Cutty Sark*, and sailing-ships, and went into steam. He had saved a little money, and he put it into a steamship company, with which he took a command. There, poor man, he lost everything, for the company failed.

Chapter Three

TRAMPING

CAPTAIN MOODIE'S decision bothered old White Hat. Good masters were becoming ever harder to find. Even at their best, some of the crack clippers were poorly commanded. The ideal combination of qualities necessary to get the best out of a racing square-rigged ship, week after week and month after month, and to make a commercial success out of her voyage into the bargain, was not often found in the person of one man. Yet one man was master, and had to be. No committees could run a sailing-ship. Consummate seamanship, magnificent leadership, iron nerves, an equable temperament and the ability to go without sleep for days on end and with insufficient rest for months, perfect judgement of wind and gear and weather and sea, mastery of a huge mass of sailing-lore painfully acquired (often its very acquisition would break down many men), the ability to withstand temptation of all sorts, especially of the bottle—these were only a few of the necessary qualities. A great clipper-captain had to have the feeling of a magnificent conductor, the brain of a tank general, infinite practical ability, unquestionable power of command, and the body of an ox. He was a master-sailmaker, master-shipwright, master-stevedore. He

was his ship's brains, eyes, thoughts, and controlling
hands.   He had complete charge of a great seafaring
entity—great though so small—in such a manner as is
not now known, and little appreciated.   No wonder
that good clipper-captains were hard to find !

Captain Moodie was succeeded in command of the
Cutty Sark by Captain F. W. Moore, who was the
Willis marine superintendent at the time.   Moore
was a great captain and had a splendid reputation,
but he was past real driving when he took over the
new command.   As marine superintendent, he hated
to see ships damaged in any way and he was most
reluctant to place too great a strain on wooden masts
and yards and hempen running rigging.   So the
Cutty Sark rarely did her best for him.   She needed
driving.   The spirit of the wanton witch could cope
with gales and heavy winds, and did not like lying
down to them.   The scream of the gale was music in
Nannie's ears, and she would tear along as if she
really were after her man, rigged down to her " cutty
sark " and ready for action.   Snugged down she sulked
a little though she still would not allow any ship to
pass her.   She did not like the sedate hand of Captain
Moore.

He had her only for one voyage.   First, she sailed
out to Melbourne with general cargo.   She left London,
very deeply laden, on November 26, 1872, and was
anchored in Port Philip Bay on February 11, 1873.
But the *Thomas Stephens* sailed a week after her and
reached Melbourne on the same day.   The *Stephens*
was lucky enough to miss a gale that the *Cutty Sark*

met in the Channel. The two ships took their departures on the same day, the *Sark* from the Lizard and the *Stephens* from Start Point. From Melbourne the clippers shifted round the coast to lift New South Wales coal for Shanghai, no less than a dozen of the crack ships taking part in this trade. The *Cutty Sark* ran up through the S.W. Pacific—up through the Coral Sea and then outside the Philippines and through the chain of the Ryukyu Islands—in 41 days, which was two days better than the *Thermopylae* did that year. But the *Hallowe'en* and the *Doune Castle* made the same run in five weeks. Coal was a heavy cargo for the clippers, and the *Cutty Sark's* powerful stern dragged her back a bit in light winds when she was deeply laden. She had to weather a typhoon near the Ladrones, but she took that in her stride. Captain Moore had her in beautiful shape alow and aloft, and even the hurricane winds failed to shift a spar, though the *Blackadder* was badly dismasted in the same blow.

This year the famous ships *Sir Lancelot, Titania, Thermopylae* and *Cutty Sark* loaded tea together in Shanghai and a wonderful race was promised, despite the steamers. These ships had to beat down the China Sea at the time of the unfavourable monsoon, and that year the weather was particularly violent. It was not just the ability to sail fast when she had a good wind that made the China tea clipper's reputation. It was her general sailing ability—her capacity to ghost along with next to no wind at all, her weatherliness, by which is chiefly meant her dexterity in

biting her way to windward against wind and sea.
It was, above all, her sailing qualities in *adverse* conditions that gave her a lead over her peers. It was of
no use merely to go outside, pick up a fair wind, and
then hang studding-sails all round the ship like
the Monday washing. Studding-sails, so beloved by
artists, were essentially fine-weather kites, morale
builders in light winds more than really useful canvas.
They looked well though they were an infernal nuisance
to set, and a worse nuisance to trim.

There was no use for such sails when the clippers
were engaged in the dour beat right down the China
Sea. Here everything was against them. There was
no hope of a fair wind, in the wrong season. Worse
than the constant head wind was the fact that it also
brought up a strong adverse current and, though the
ships might avoid the worst of this by getting over
on the western side, the waters were badly charted—
they still are—full of reefs and sets, and shallows and
all sorts of traps for the deep hulls of sailing-ships.
There were many narrow straits to beat through, and
nothing but dour slogging to wind'ard could get a
ship past such places. There was no other way she
could go. So day and night, day after day and week
after week, the little ships would beat and fight their
way along against rising wind and short steep sea,
and rain and poor visibility with the chance of a stray
typhoon until they got well down. It was more than
a chance. The *Cutty Sark* had to fight another
typhoon this passage, near Formosa. She came
through all right, but it set her back, and she was

twelve days astern of the *Thermopylae* by the time she reached Anjer. Kemball of the *Thermopylae* was always noted for the splendid passages he made down the China Sea, no matter what the season. He must have been a magnificent shipmaster.

Moore brought the *Cutty Sark* home that year in 117 days. It might have been worse. But the *Thermopylae* beat him by more than a fortnight, and the *Hallowe'en* was only 90 days. It is fair to add that the *Hallowe'en* sailed over four months after the others and had a favourable monsoon down the China Sea —a very different story, indeed. The old-timers never spoke of a tea clipper's passage without mentioning the time of year she passed through the China Sea, for it was obviously unjust to compare the passage of a ship which romped along before a soldier's wind with others which had had to beat the first 2,000 miles —and *knew it*, when they sailed. The difficulties of that beat were well known and indeed, Lloyd's underwriters generally charged higher premiums on ships which chanced it. This was offset by the ships' better freights. The *Cutty Sark*, for instance, had tea at £4 for each 50 cubic feet, and the *Hallowe'en's* freight was only £2 10s. So it made sense to buck the wrong monsoon.

Captain Moore was followed by Captain W. E. Tiptaft, who seems to have been a modest and competent seaman, but without the verve of the true racing master. He had not commanded a real clipper before, and he appears to have taken things a bit easy in the *Cutty Sark*. He took her to Sydney first

—for Sydney was a handier port for a coal charter on to China—and his log indicates that he was reluctant to go much south of Forty South in his quest of west winds. The *Thermopylae* went down to Forty-five and Forty-seven and raced to Melbourne in 72 days, which was a week better than Tiptaft's time to Sydney. Most of the tea clippers went down to Australia that year, for the steamers by then were taking almost all the general cargo to China. There was plenty of business for the sailers on the loading berth to Melbourne and Sydney, and the coal business to Chinese ports was also doing well. The increasing number of steamers made considerable, and growing, demands for bunker coal, and the sailing-ships brought it for them—not willingly. They hated coal cargoes almost as much as they hated steamers. But it was business. It was obviously cheaper to stock Pacific bunker ports with coal from New South Wales than to ship the stuff from the United Kingdom. So the sailing-ships would arrive at Shanghai having already earned two freights, and there was still a good profit to be made from them.

There was no tea at Shanghai for the *Cutty Sark*, and for a while it was thought she might have to go back to Australia, empty, to bring more coal. However her China coast agents—Jardine, Matheson— were enterprising fellows, not so greatly carried away by the obviously increasing steamship business that they threw the clippers on the discard. So they sent the little ship 600 miles up the Yangtze-kiang to load new season's tea at Hankow. Their London

The *Cutty Sark* in a fresh monsoon.   (*From a painting.*)

Two of Captain Woodget's famous collie dogs.   He reared
them in the *Cutty Sark*.

A picture of the *Cutty Sark* taken by Captain Woodget (inset).

correspondents were still writing them that the London market would pay well enough for a few clipper cargoes brought round the Cape, even though the tea was a month longer at sea—at least—than in any steamer. The old myth that it was better carried in sail was still much alive, and the *Cutty Sark* was able to get her Hankow cargo without much difficulty. Hankow was a dangerous place to load, with swift currents, and mudbanks, and plenty of jagged rocks —and a 600-mile tow to pay for, too, both ways.

Tiptaft, by loading at Hankow, was able to bring the first sail-carried new season's tea to the London market. But he did not hurry over it. There were several ways down the China Sea, and the more dangerous were the faster. He took the easiest way and was 118 days to London. Again, the *Thermopylae* beat him by a fortnight. The redoubtable Kemball was still in command of the Aberdeen ship, but it was his last voyage in her. He left when she arrived home, to take over the iron clipper *Aristides*, a green beauty of a ship which also was to achieve great fame in the Australian trade.

The *Cutty Sark*, though she was beaten so roundly by her old rival, made a better passage than most of the other racers. Again, when the tea cargo was out, she sailed to Australia and made the best passage of 1874–75 to Sydney. This was 73 days : but the *Thermopylae* was only 64 days to Melbourne. Again, it was the chance of a fair wind down-channel, where the *Cutty Sark* had had to slog against a south-west gale and lost a man washed overboard, that gave the

other ship the edge. If one ship sailed a week ahead
of another and then had to spend that week beating
against an appalling head wind, which had blown
itself out and been replaced by a favouring wind by
the time the second ship sailed, then of course the
later sailing ship had a very great advantage. Though
her hull might never move through the water any
faster than her rival's, though her master, officers and
crew were of equal abilities and she had nothing
whatever else in her favour, she might well make the
better passage through luck and not merit, and win
the "race". It was for this reason that the old-
timers paid heed only when ships left the same port,
in the same trim, on the same tide. It was just because
the *Cutty Sark* continued, voyage after voyage, to
miss slight initial advantages which the *Thermopylae*
had the luck to gain, that the rivalry between the two
ships remained at a high pitch and old Willis continued doggedly to believe that he had, after all, the
better ship. Had he? The point is still arguable.
At any rate, it is certain that he had no Kemball for
his clipper until it was almost too late. Tiptaft did
well, but not well enough. He picked up new season's
tea again at Hankow, but was over four months
delivering it to London. Once again, the *Thermopylae*
beat her—this time by almost a week. But the ships
did not sail from the same port nor at the same time.
The *Hallowe'en* was only 92 days.

The *Cutty Sark* was back at London on October 21,
1875. A month later to the day, she sailed for Sydney.
On this passage she ran 2,163 miles in six consecutive

days, in the Roaring Forties : but at the same time
the *Thermopylae*, which had sailed almost a week after
her, was romping along at an average 270 miles a day.
Again the rival had the better passage, this time by
a week. The *Thermopylae* went to Melbourne, as
usual, and the *Cutty Sark's* Sydney supporters pointed
out that it was further to their port, and—according
to them, at any rate—if she had only been bound to
Melbourne, the *Cutty Sark* would have arrived there
only 64 days out. Perhaps she would, for she was
certainly in Bass Straits at that time and *could* have
made Melbourne Heads when the wind forced her to
turn and head towards the south of Tasmania.

The log line—a contrivance of high quality light
hemp, marked with knots up to 15½, which used to
be paid out from a reel held in the hands of two
large apprentices—often ran out its full length before
the sand was all out of the glass, during that run.
The clipper's speed was computed at 17 knots or
possibly a shade better, and that was a wonderful
speed for a deeply-laden ship with a waterline of little
more than 200 feet. Neither she nor the *Thermopylae*,
nor any other of the tea clippers, had the great advantage of the big passenger ships in the Australian
run, like the wonderful *Lightning* and the *James
Baines*, the *Sobraon* and the rest. These kept their
'tween-decks empty of cargo to give the passengers
room to sleep, and so they were always comparatively
lightly loaded. This meant both that there was less
of their hulls immersed and so needing to be driven
through the water, and their decks were up out of

the sea and drier and safer. They could be pressed even more than the clippers were.

After all, it made no sense to sail a clipper under. If too great a weight of water ever descended at once on her decks from the great snarling seas in which she raced, she most certainly would go under. Some did. Many had narrow escapes. They were very much *in* the sea, and they had no great reserve of buoyancy. Neither the name of the *Cutty Sark* nor of the *Thermopylae* appears in the list, published in Lloyd's Calendar, of sailing-ships claiming the greatest day's runs. These are all larger clippers, designed as passenger ships for the Australian run —the Black Ball Line's *Champion of the Seas*, which said she made good 20 knots one day in December, 1854, to complete a day's noon-to-noon run between observations of 465 miles ; the *Lightning*, the *Donald MacKay*, *James Baines*, *Great Republic*, and *Sovereign of the Seas*, all of which claimed day's runs of more than 400 miles. These ships were built by Donald MacKay. Yet it is curious that it is the *Thermopylae* which holds the record for the London-to-Melbourne run, and the *Cutty Sark* is very little behind her. It is the *Thermopylae*, again, which holds the record—28 days— from Newcastle to Shanghai. And the *Cutty Sark's* 67-day run from Sydney to the Channel in 1885 is very little behind the *Lightning's* record 63 days from Melbourne to Liverpool, though the *Lightning* was over twice her tonnage.

The difficulty with a deep-loaded little ship, trying to race before a gale, was that continuous gales brought

Mizzen mast and poop of the *Cutty Sark*.

The *Cutty Sark* was dismasted more than once. But always she sailed again.

The figurehead was of a witch, from a Burns poem.

The sleek cutwater of the *Cutty Sark,* and the graceful bows.

The *Cutty Sark* as the Portuguese *Ferreira,* rigged temporarily as a barquentine.

up seas that she could not survive in, for if she were driven too hard the seas would race over her. A big ship with more freeboard could run much longer. If a sailing-ship once began to take seas badly over her stern or roll them in over both quarters, she was finished.

Under Captain Tiptaft, there was little chance that the *Cutty Sark* would sail under. She went from Australia up to China again, with coal and, after that was discharged, loaded tea again at Hankow. Tiptaft made a splendid passage home and beat the *Thermopylae* by a week. She had the better freight, too—£4 5s. as against the other's £3. Altogether it was an excellent round voyage, and old White Hat was very pleased.

But the Glen Line's steamer *Glenartney* had her tea home in six weeks, and so did the *Glenearn*, and a dozen other steamers. Though there was still thought to be room for a sailing-ship parcel or two brought round the Cape, it was becoming increasingly difficult to maintain the idea or to get a decent rate for bringing the tea. Others of the surviving clippers had begun to take silk as well as tea, and altogether, only eight of them loaded in China in '76, full or part cargoes. The *Titania* went to New York from Shanghai and the lovely *Sir Lancelot* ran out to Otago and thence to Yokohama to load for France. Tea was all but finished as a cargo for clippers, or any other kind of sailing-ship. Loading costs were high, and the clippers had always been accustomed to wait for a cargo. A cargo worth waiting for had to pay

D

a good freight, and since the steamers could time
their voyages to arrive when the cargo was pretty
well ready, they could afford to undercut. Moreover,
they were well stowed with other goods, and did not
have to buy ballast, or waste good paying space on
its stowage. A clipper has to be in perfect trim to
do her best ; a steamer could hog along with a hog's
load, and make a good enough passage of it.

Old Willis did not speak of " bought winds " any
longer, though he continued to hope that the Suez
Canal would cave in. The Canal Company, however,
was doing very well, and the canal was splendidly
maintained. The clippers' hopes now lay almost
entirely in the maintenance of the fiction that tea
carried round Good Hope in their hulls reached the
market in better condition than tea carried in the
steamers. Tea, however, was steadily becoming more
and more a popular beverage, and the number of
consumers who could distinguish between sail-carried
and steam-carried tea—or who imagined they could—
was diminishing. Tea was available at lower prices,
too. There was no hope that clipper freights would
ever rise again, even if the sailers could get a cargo.

The *Cutty Sark* had her last China tea cargo in '77.
She cleared from Woosung—after loading up-river at
Hankow—on June 6 that year, but it was not until
127 days later that she arrived in the Thames. The
Thermopylae had sailed a month later, but was along-
side in London only a week after her. The *Cutty
Sark's* freight had to cover her river towage costs
over 1,500 miles, and the cost of two good anchors

left in the deep mud of the Yangtze. Some of the
clippers had had to take £2. There were poor dividends that year, and plenty of pessimism. But the
old personal shipowners were courageous old bull-
dogs who did not know when they were beaten.
Willis refused to accept the obvious. He put his
best clipper on the loading berth for Sydney again,
and once more, she raced out in less than two and a
half months.

But first she was very nearly wrecked on the Good-
wins the day after she left London. She was caught
in an exceptionally violent November gale which
flung squalls of hurricane force at her. Compelled
to shelter in the Downs, she was one of scores of
ships which could not keep their ground tackle in the
furious storm. In the days of sail, casualties were
much more commonplace than they are to-day. Ships
were exposed to much greater risks near the land.
Unable to beat against the terrific wind and unable
to shelter or keep her anchors in the turbulent seas
even in the Downs, she drove about helplessly. It
was a black night, and the Downs was full of driving
ships, crashing into one another, driving on the sands,
sinking, capsizing, sending up distress flares. Every
lifeboat on the east coast of England went out that
night, and the surf breaking on the Kent beaches in
the morning rolled the bodies of drowned seamen on
the sand. Once, twice, the *Cutty Sark*, driving helpless, collided with unknown ships, crunching and
grinding together, smashing each other's yards and
long jib-booms. Tiptaft tried to get sail on the

clipper, but her canvas soon lashed to ribbons. Her bulwarks were stove in and much of her running rigging was cut away by the collisions. It was in the nick of time that the tug *McGregor* got hold of her in the morning and, even then, could barely hold her off the sands. A second tug had to help before the crippled ship could at last be brought safely back into the Thames.

This was salvage. The two tugs claimed £8,000. The value of the ship and cargo was put at £85,000. With an award of £3,000 the tugs were not overpaid. But it was a costly night. Other ships which had been damaged sued the *Cutty Sark* as the ship— they said—that collided with them. But they couldn't prove it. One at least of them might have been able to, for her name-board fell into the clipper's scuppers while the ships were locked together. The carpenter, an old man who had been in the ship since she was launched, saw the name-board lying there in the morning and quietly threw it overboard, without a word to any-one. He wasn't going to have his beloved ship paying out money to any strange vessel, especially to one which had damaged her. It wasn't until many years afterwards that he admitted what he had done.

When she finally reached Sydney, the *Cutty Sark* discharged her general cargo, and at once took in coal for Shanghai. While she had been storming out to Sydney, her great rival had run magnificently from the Lizard to the Line in seventeen days, though she was 74 days London to Melbourne compared with the *Cutty's* 72 to Sydney. When the little group of surviving clippers reached Shanghai, it was to find that what little tea was left for them could pay a freight of only 25 or 35 shillings. This was ruinous. The *Cutty Sark* managed to get half a cargo at Hankow and then shifted to Shanghai, hoping to complete. This she could not do, for there was no more tea there. So the Hankow parcel was discharged, and she went tramping with coal cargoes across to Japan. Back again in Shanghai, still no tea was offering. The season was a bad one, and there was nothing like the usual quantity of tea on the market and, in any event, the steamers had taken almost all of it. The *Thermopylae* took a cargo, at 35s. for the standard 50 cubic feet, and was home in 110 days.

While the *Cutty Sark* was waiting, Captain Tiptaft died. He was succeeded in command by his mate, Captain Wallace. This was towards the end of '78. Tiptaft had done well in bad times. He had shown what the little ship could do, especially in the Australian trade. He had nursed her and looked after her well, and made quite tolerable passages. But Wallace was a real driver.

Chapter Four

A BUCKO MATE, AND OTHER EVILS

WALLACE might have been a driver, but there was no tea to be driven, and after hanging about Shanghai for months, the *Cutty Sark* had to sail back to Sydney in ballast. This costly and time-wasting sort of thing was only a taste of the fate awaiting sailing-ships, although they were to be built in the United Kingdom for another quarter of a century and, in Germany, for almost half a century. The new sailing-ships were not small, however, and very few of them were racers. One thing they all had in common which such vessels as the tea clippers lacked. They had great dead-weight capacity. They could carry a lot, and earn good money when freights were offering. The day of the luxury cargo-carrier and racing passenger sailing-ship was definitely over. The crews which handled such vessels as the *Cutty Sark* were large enough to handle vessels three times her size. The clipper's complement was 28 men, all of them—at first—skilled and fearless seamen. When, in later days, Willis cut her crew to 23 and 24, and even at times to 19, that was the same number which handled big four-masted barques carrying anything up to 5,000 tons of cargo. If sailing-ships were forced out of the luxury trades, they had to carry what

54

offered—bulk cargoes like wheat and lumber, and rice, and nitrates.

At any rate Wallace made a good passage down to Sydney. Sailing *from* Sydney to Shanghai was a comparatively easy romp up before the trade winds, up through the Coral Sea and the Western Pacific—a flying-fish passage. But going *to* Sydney was a different affair altogether, for the square-rigged ship had first to work her way down the South China Sea (just as if she were bound to Europe), then through the breadth of the Indian Ocean, and then run her easting down—as they called it—across the stormy seas south of Australia and sail up the east coast, coming into Sydney from the south. Wallace had the little ship off Anjer just over a fortnight after leaving Shanghai and passed south of Tasmania when he had been six weeks at sea. He was seven weeks to Sydney.

Still sticking to that optimistic and ill-founded belief that his thoroughbred could find tea to carry, old Willis ordered the clipper to take coal back to Shanghai and this she did, with a good passage of a little over six weeks. Again it was futile. The *Thermopylae* did not even try the market, but contented herself with a cargo of Australian wool which she took homewards round the Horn, and that was the first time either of those great ships—*Cutty Sark* and *Thermopylae*—rounded Cape Horn. It was far from the last.

Wallace took the clipper to Manila to load jute and sugar for New York, which she reached after a passage of 111 days. Then she ran back to the Thames in 19 days. According to her crew, it was only ten days from off Sandy Hook, but the log does not uphold this. Maybe the crew's idea of "off Sandy Hook" was a few hundred miles off, out in the Atlantic. Clipper crews never belittled their ships or their performances. Even as late as 1952 there was a *Cutty Sark* survivor who declared that she had sailed from the Channel to Cape Otway in 54 days, and from the Lizard to the Line in 16, though such records were never claimed by her masters or by Willis. Nor are they in her logs. According to the same informant, the ship was "never passed by anything, not even an albatross"—or, one supposes, by a four-jet air-liner. If by strange chance such an apparition *had* caught up with her, no one aboard would have looked.

At this stage in their affairs the surviving clippers were dispersed. Some went to the Indian coastal trade, some to the trans-Pacific. Even old White Hat had become a pessimist. No longer did he spend money freely to maintain the pride of his fleet. He reduced her rig, cutting down her heavy spars on the plea that her racing days were over. This was one of the best things he ever did, though his reason was proved gloriously wrong. Most clippers were unnecessarily over-sparred. They could afford to be reduced a bit, and such airy kites as sky sails taken from them. On a 15,000-mile haul it was doubtful if a skysail made half an hour's difference, and its weight added considerably to the strain on the main topgallantmast. Even studding-sails were usually more nuisance than they were worth, and the designers who incorporated sufficient of their area into broad double topsails and double topgallants did seafarers a good turn. Of course, the old-timers kicked at every innovation. They scorned even double tops'ls for a quarter of a century, and used to leave the upper yard mastheaded because they held that the double yards spoiled the look of their ships. Even in 1952, one full-rigged schoolship was still rigged like that, because her predecessor had been a single tops'l frigate, and her master liked things the way they were.

So there were plenty of kicks when the *Cutty Sark's* rig was cut down a little, even from those whose work was very much lightened by that change for the better. Shortly after her rig had been reduced, the ship was chartered to load best steam coal in the Bristol Channel, for the American Navy in Chinese waters. Naval ships were finely strung then, as now, and nothing but the best steam coal was good enough for them. So off went the little ship round to Penarth to lift her first coal cargo from a U.K. port. Her reduced rig and circumstances were, unfortunately, reflected in her crew. The days were gone when clippers could command loyalty from the best class of mariners. Now, like other sailing-ships, they had to take what they could get. There was, moreover, a great demand for good, steady officers in the steamships, which by that time were doing very well in all the passenger trades —across the North Atlantic, to South Africa, to Australia—as well as in the cargo business. New great steamship lines were being formed, and they all required both mariners and officers.

So it happened that the crew the *Cutty Sark* was furnished for that voyage was a poor one. Worse than that, the officers were a poor lot, too. The mate was something of a " Bucko "—which is another name for bully—and the second mate was a weak type. He had poor eyesight, too, and could scarcely see clearly from the poop to the fore royal yard. Captain Wallace was a good man and an excellent sailor, but he had one fatal weakness. He was too easy-going. He lacked the essential qualities of leadership. He did not put his bucko in his place as he should have done. Instead, he suffered him. The crew, shipped at Penarth, perhaps was the better for a little bullying the first week out. But it went on for months.

Wallace did another foolish thing. He sailed on a Friday. This may seem a small thing, but in 1880, and for many years afterwards, it was flying in the face of all maritime tradition. Sailors before the mast were superstitious, and they were appalled at the idea of sailing on a Friday. It was *tabu*. It was just not done. They held the belief, firmly and against all possible argument, that to begin a voyage —any voyage—on a Friday was to fly in the face of Providence. They lived by the grace of Providence, and they were well aware of that. A man took his life in his own strong hands when he shipped away in a long-voyage clipper or any other kind of deep-sea sailing-ship. To begin the voyage by deliberately flouting such an ancient superstition was to ask for disloyalty. Wallace asked for it. And he got it.

Included in the crew were eight apprentices, good stout lads, who, after a year or two in the ship, were as competent as most able seamen. Their parents had paid premiums for them to be taught the business of seafaring, and it was incidental that the lads also provided a solid core of cheap, efficient, and completely loyal labour. It was a good thing they were there. The foremast hands were a ragged lot, including several who had not been in that class of ship previously, and a notorious old croaker who went by the name of Vanderdecken. Sailing on a Friday horrified this man, and he forecast every imaginable kind of accident. He kept on forecasting accidents throughout the whole of his stay in the ship, and, unfortunately, too many of his forecasts were accurate.

But at first the *Cutty Sark* raced along very well, after an initial setback from a south-west gale, and she was well on the way to making a splendid passage when she reached the south-east trades of the Indian Ocean. The Bucko mate at least had the crew working well, though one steamer hand named Francis, a coloured man, remained completely recalcitrant and useless. When a hard-driven clipper, already shorthanded, shipped men who were no use aloft, of course a great strain was thrown on all the others. Francis was not popular either in the forecastle or abaft the mast, and the Bucko mate went out of his way to haze him.

This was in accordance with the traditions of the

sea of those days.   Vanderdecken had no fault to find
with this.   But he continued to expect the ship to
be dismasted, to run into icebergs in the Roaring
Forties or to collide with the island of St. Paul, to
lose a watch overboard, to spring a serious leak—in
short, to be overtaken by severe calamity sooner or
later.   He never ceased expounding these views, and,
after a time, they began to get on his shipmates'
nerves.   Vanderdecken was one of that strange class
of seafarer, now extinct, who were supremely competent working seamen, born helmsmen and absolute
wizards in the rigging, and yet were unable to sleep
or to mix properly with their shipmates at all.   In
six square-rigged ships in my youth I knew only
one such man, and he was a severe trial.   He paced
the deck when he should have been asleep, waiting
for the calamity he was sure would happen and
determined that he at least would be ready for it.
And ready he was, at all hours of the day and night.
The little iron barque we sailed in *had* sprung a
serious leak and all but foundered.   It was common
knowledge aboard that the old man had once been
in a lifeboat for weeks and weeks where cannibalism
had been practised, and it was thought he was one of
the cannibals.   This might have explained his difficulty in living with himself.

What dreadful background old Vanderdecken in
the *Cutty Sark* may have had no one can now say,
for no records remain of any other voyages the man
made.   But his croaking and the mate's bullying had
an unnerving effect on the crew.   It was a pity.

Captain Wallace was respected and the second mate's watch was a happy one. If either the Bucko or Vanderdecken had been absent, the ship would probably have kept out of trouble.

In the better weather of the Indian Ocean the coloured man, Francis, became impossible. He had already had one battle with the mate earlier in the voyage. One morning, when a course alteration made it necessary to square the yards, Francis was on lookout. The lookout's duties included tending the gear on the forecastle-head, as might be necessary during bracing, and so forth. When the yards of a sailing-ship were trimmed there was a great deal of work to be done, for the set of all the sails was altered. The lookout should look after the fore-tack, which was usually taken to the capstan on the forecastle-head. When the yards were being squared in the tack had to be eased. It was a simple job, calling neither for skill nor much muscular effort.

The crojack and the mainyards were squared in without trouble. The watch hurried along to the fore braces.

"On the lookout there! Slack away the tack!" the mate shouted.

No answer came. Nothing was done.

"Lookout there! Ease away the tack!"

No answer. No action.

Now, no mate or second mate, or third mate or bos'n or any other person entrusted with the working of a sailing-ship, bucko or otherwise, could tolerate this sort of thing. It was not only insubordination.

It was incipient mutiny. Failure to carry out any order promptly and efficiently could jeopardise a full-rigged ship and all aboard. One tradition could not be flouted, and that was the immediate obedience of *any* orders.

The mate, breathing fire, made a rush for the forecastle-head. Whoever was there was for it.

It was Francis, though the mate hadn't known that until he saw the wretched man. Just what happened in the next few seconds will never be known. The story is, that Francis was lying in wait with a capstan-bar and some crazy idea of braining the mate. But the mate seized the bar from him and promptly brained him. At any rate Francis was dead.

The ship was in an uproar. Francis dead was more trouble than Francis alive, and Vanderdecken stirred the hands to a state of undeclared mutiny. The mate locked himself in his cabin and Captain Wallace took his watch. So the clipper raced on with her good steam coal and, shortly afterwards, raised the coast of Java. Unfortunately the ship had to wait at anchor off Anjer for orders as to which port to deliver the coal, and Wallace foolishly allowed the mate to run. If the mate had faced his trial there would have been a good chance that his act of man-slaughter would have been condoned as necessary for the safety of the ship. Running away did no one any good. It was followed by open mutiny as soon as the crew discovered it. They refused to do a hand's turn aboard the ship. Wallace began at once to sail the ship with the apprentices and petty officers.

But as soon as she entered the Java she ran into an absolute state of calm which continued for three days.

Calm is the great curse of sailing-ships. Poor Wallace showed the strain dreadfully. He never left the deck. The calm got on his nerves. All day long the ship lay silent upon the image of herself reflected in the sullen sea ; by night the garbage that had been flung overboard at dusk stayed with her, not moving. Not a sail flapped. The ship lay lifeless where she should have been speeding before a favouring wind. Vanderdecken croaked about in whispers, and his bare feet padded upon the teak decks night after night—all night. He reduced many of the crew almost to a state of terror.

"You see ; you see !" he croaked. "She can't go now. She *can't* go ! There's a curse on her, that's what I say !"

The fact that he had been saying the same thing for years, aboard every ship he'd been in, was irrelevant. The calm was eerie, oppressive, and foreboding.

At four o'clock in the morning on the fourth day of calm, Captain Wallace walked over the side. They put out a boat at once, but nothing was seen of him again. Almost at once a faint breath of air got up and began to grow. The *Cutty Sark* was sailing again. But where to go ? The second mate was now in charge. All he had to do was to coax the ship along on the fine-weather run to Yokohama. What a chance for a young man ! But the second mate lacked both the competence and the nerve. Poor wretch, his bad eyesight bothered him and he had been unnerved by the hazing in the ship, and, above all, by Wallace's sudden death. He had plenty of able lieutenants in the apprentices' quarters if he had the nerve to use them and the courage to rely upon them. More than one very junior officer and some apprentices distinguished themselves in similar circumstances in the days of sail by taking over command and bringing their ships safely to the completion of their voyages.

This second mate was not in that mould, unfortunately. He returned to Anjer, anchored, and promptly began to bombard the owner in London with long cables which made nothing clear except that the poor ship was in a great deal of trouble. Willis ordered him on to Yokohama (for the freight on that Navy coal was good, but it had to be delivered to the Navy). He might as well have ordered him to hell. It was a pity indeed, that the second mate had not run with the mate, or jumped over the side with his captain. Then one of the senior apprentices could have taken the ship. Several were quite competent. Wallace had taken a keen interest in their welfare and professional abilities, and most of them were quite good navigators.

The upshot was that a still mystified Willis had finally to order the *Cutty Sark* to Singapore in charge of a Dutch pilot. On the way dead calm again cursed the ship, and at one stage she was swept in a tidal race so close by the rocky cliffs of Thwart-the-Way Island that the yards had to be braced sharp up to avoid scraping the rocks.

The sharp lines of the old ship show up in dry dock.

Circular Quay, Sydney, 1871.   This was where the
wool-clippers loaded.

Main deck view, the *Cutty Sark* as restored by Captain W. H. Dowman.

The steering wheel and binnacle.

The restored *Cutty Sark* towing from Falmouth to London, in 1938.

At Singapore, Vanderdecken promptly left, vowing
that his life's work would be to track down the bucko
mate and bring him to "justice." On the face of it,
Venderdecken's quest seemed hopeless. There is
little doubt that the bucko mate got away in an
American ship which was lying off Anjer with the
Cutty Sark. But sailing-ship sailors were nothing if
not inveterate globe-wanderers. It is certainly a fact
that the bucko, whose name was Smith, *was* recog-
nised by a member of the *Cutty Sark's* crew—said
to be Vanderdecken—years afterwards, and he *was*
brought to trial. Basil Lubbock—that fine sailing-
ship historian—give an account of it in an appendix
to his classic " Log of the *Cutty Sark.*"* Smith was
tried, under the name of John Anderson, for the
wilful murder of John Francis, at the Central Criminal
Court in London. It was brought out in evidence
that he had acted under great provocation and the
charge was reduced to manslaughter. On this he was
found guilty and, despite the fact that several witnesses who had known him many years testified to
his good character and generally humane disposition,
he was sentenced to seven years' penal servitude.

Among the character witnesses was John Willis,
who did the best he could for his former mate. Smith,
alias Anderson, or Anderson alias Smith, served his
time helping to build the Dover breakwater. When
he was released he went back to sea at once. He
had lost his certificates, of course, but Willis got him
a berth as bosun and second mate of a square-rigger

* Brown, Son and Ferguson, Glasgow.

E

bound to Australia. Bucko or not, Smith showed he had plenty of courage. He worked his way again through the Board of Trade's certificates of competency, taking his second mate, mate, and master as soon as he could. He rose to command with the Anglo-American Oil Company, which retired him on a pension for his good service. He died of cancer in 1922, when he was nearly seventy-five years old.

What happened to Vanderdecken no man knows.

When the *Cutty Sark* reached Singapore on that tragic voyage her troubles were far from over. There she was in that hotbed of the East, without a competent officer aboard, or a crew. (The foremast hands had soon melted away.) Willis, not wishing to send a new master out in a despised steamship, cabled to the master of the *Hallowe'en* at Hong Kong asking whether the mate of that ship could be recommended for command. It so happened that the master hated the mate and would have recommended him for anything to get rid of him. So off went the mate post haste to Singapore to take over his first command. A worse choice could hardly have been made, and that master of the *Hallowe'en* has a lot to answer for. The new captain's name was Bruce, and he was the worst possible type of man to command a full-blooded clipper. The *Cutty Sark* scared him into a state of nervous prostration which he covered alternately by drink and an air of tremendous rectitude. This air he kept for shore consumption ; the ship and her people soon found him out.

Bruce was a small man with an unctuous countenance and large, protruding eyes. A slobbery mouth and a high-pitched tenor voice, a false cheerfulness ashore and a real capacity for villainy and petty bullying aboard combined to make him the laughing-stock of his own apprentices, and he knew it. He was a man who found himself extremely hard to live with, and he was for ever trying to make up for his appalling shortcomings by acts of silly braggadocio or senseless swaggering which everyone saw through, including himself. He was happy only in drink or in psalm-singing ashore, and there was considerable doubt about the psalm-singing. He certainly was a most extraordinary man. In the various ports of call, shore people thought kindly of him. He was asked to conduct services, and once a collection was made and a gold watch presented to him, as a mark of esteem for his great " piety ". Yet aboard the ship he was a petulant little tyrant, covering his fear of the ship by tremulous shouting at the crew and petty fault-finding of his officers. One thing he feared even more than the ship, and that was land-falls. Any landfalls. Any land, indeed, anywhere. The man was a splendid navigator and had less cause to fear his landfalls indeed than many of his fellow shipmasters. But he seemed quite incapable of rousing any self-confidence. Whenever the ship was approaching land he became quite unnerved, and often hove her to, wasting time stupidly, rather than trust himself and let her stand on to pick up the land. He dreaded coming into port ; perhaps he hated to put on his shore-going manners and to pretend to be a psalm-singer.

Under the ignoble Bruce, the poor ship wandered about the seven seas, tramping for cargoes. Sometimes he was so drunk that she ran away with him like the wanton she was, and when he hove her to, near the land, she kicked and bucked like a recalcitrant mule. From Singapore she went to Calcutta where, after several months of waiting, she loaded Indian tea for Melbourne. It was perhaps ironic that the clipper, forced out of her rightful business of carrying China tea, now opened up the great Australian market to the Indian product, and then had no further share in carrying that. This cargo of the *Cutty Sark's* was the first Indian tea ever shipped to Australia, where it soon became a popular beverage. From Australia the *Cutty Sark* took coal to China again ; thence to Cebu for jute to deliver in New York. Owing to Bruce's goings on, the ship was out of food long before she reached the American port, and the proud little clipper was forced to beg provisions from passing ships. This was inexcusable. The only reason for the ship's shortage was the misuse of the funds provided by the owner for buying food, for Willis liked to see that his ships were properly stored.

In New York at last, Bruce found a port where a faked appearance of sanctity did him no good at all. Between the bottle and the Bible-punching he broke down, and at last was removed from the ship.

It was just in time. Any more of Bruce and buckos, and the clipper might as well have gone up in flames.

Chapter Five

CAPTAIN WOODGET

WITH the *Cutty Sark* stuck without a crew and without officers in the expensive port of New York, Willis was in a dilemma. The ship was already loading a full cargo of case-oil for Samarang, and a crew she must have. New York was a bad place for crews, then, and a worse for officers. Willis solved his difficulties by robbing another of his ships, the clipper *Blackadder*, which happened also to be in New York at the time. He took her master, mate, and crew, almost complete, across to the *Cutty Sark*.

The master of the *Blackadder* at the time was a Captain F. Moore—no relation to the other Moore who had the *Cutty Sark* earlier—a thoroughly experienced and capable seaman, and a good disciplinarian as well. He found the old tea clipper in a disgraceful state. Bruce had not been content to rob his owner only on the provisions. He had skimped the ship in every possible way and generally neglected her. Sails, running rigging, and even some of the standing rigging were alike in poor condition. She needed thousands spending on her, but there was little prospect of earning thousands with the freight of case-oil— a rather desperate one for such a fine-lined ship—and Willis clamped down. His orders were that expenses must be kept down to the irreducible minimum. She paid her dues, paid to have her cargo stowed—that could not be avoided—paid for pilotage out, and that was about all.

Case-oil was indeed a desperate cargo for the ship. In the first place, she was unfitted to carry it. Case-oil—really it was *cased* oil—was the trade name for the old-fashioned square cans of kerosene and the like which used to be stowed two to a wooden case. In the early days of the oil trade before bulk installations, almost all oil and oil products were handled in this way, for distant markets. To handle it, ships should be built of metal and properly ventilated. The *Cutty Sark*, never having been intended to touch such stuff, was not properly ventilated. Case-oil could be jammed by the score-thousand cases into the box-like holds of more modern ships. But her hold was more or less triangular both for'ard and aft, and was not box-like at all. If times had been good, she would have run—if necessary in ballast—back to London to load general cargo for the Far East or for Australia. But times were far from good. There was no chance of a general cargo for her to China, and the steamers were taking most of the Australian cargoes as well.

So the little ship went off with her case-oil cargo and raced down both Atlantics, round the Cape, and across the Roaring Forties, through the Indian Ocean and up to Samarang. She would have raced better had she been in better order. Captain Moore's log of that passage is a sad commentary on her condition. Sails blew out, gear carried away, avoidable grief of all kinds harassed her the whole long way. But still she skipped along when she could, as if anxious to get the case-oil delivered and the reek of paraffin out of herself for ever.

From Samarang she sailed in ballast to Madras and lifted a cargo of Eastern goods such as jaggery, myrobolanes, and buffaloes' horns, from the roadsteads at Bimlipatam and Coconada. At any rate there was no shortage of sweetening stuff that passage, for the jaggery never stopped oozing a treacly kind of molasses which had to be pumped out from the bilges. When the taint of paraffin was out of it, this stuff went quite well in the apprentices' self-made dishes. They used to pound up hard biscuits with a belaying-pin, or a capstan-bar, and mix the mess with old fat and jaggery-juice, and then shove it in the cook's oven to get hot. Probably only a sailing-ship apprentice could appreciate the result, but aboard the *Cutty Sark* it was something of a delicacy that passage. It may also have been a necessity for growing boys, for the food was not served out lavishly. Pea soup, boiled salt horse, the occasional piece of salt pork and preserved meat warmed up for Sunday dinner—this was the weekly round. Breakfast was burgoo—a watery porridge with a flavouring of weevils—and supper was whatever could be saved from the other two meals, if anything. It was for this meal that the jaggery juice and the smashed-up biscuits came in handy.

The *Cutty Sark* was a little over four months to the Channel from Coconada Roads. She did not hurry. Captain Moore was busy the whole voyage getting her properly seaworthy again and, by the time she docked in London in June, 1883, the little ship was in good condition once again, on deck and aloft. Her wonderful hull had never given any trouble. But Moore had difficulty inducing his owner to put up enough money to give the ship all the canvas and cordage she needed for another voyage, and again she went to sea rather parish-rigged. Willis was becoming a pessimist. So long as he believed his ship could capture the record in the China tea trade, he lavished money on her. But by 1883 he knew that this was out of the question. The ship was fourteen years' old, and the big iron clippers in the Australian trade were almost as much a menace as the steamers had been in the Eastern run. Nor was there the slightest sign that the Suez Canal would silt up. So old White Hat did not boast very much about his *Cutty Sark*, did not expect much from her, and began to cut down her expenses as severely as he could. As an old ship-master himself, he knew how to be a shade too severe in this direction.

Captain Moore took the *Cutty Sark* on two Australian round voyages, going out in 1883 with a general cargo to Newcastle and coming home again round the Horn. He did extremely well, so well that he made old Willis sit up. He sailed out from the Channel in 79 days, and was home again from Newcastle in 82, making not only the best passage of the ships which sailed about the same time, but the best wool passage of the year. She beat most of the other ships by anything between a fortnight and a month. This was a highly creditable performance. No one had believed that the little tea clipper could sail as well as that. Tea clippers were a bit fine-lined for the Cape Horn run, as a rule. The fact was that Willis's powerful stern and strong rigging were paying off at last. The clipper he'd hoped would beat all-comers in the tea trade years before was at last showing her real merits, in a trade for which she had not been designed. Her power and grace, her strong Scots hull and her good sail-plan combined to make her queen of the Cape Horn wool race, where she had never been intended to run at all. It was an odd quirk that made the ship a record-beater in her middle-age.

It might have been an odd quirk of fate, but she certainly was consistent. Nor was the best passage of the year a mere matter for congratulating the master and his crew. It meant money, for wool was auctioned only at certain times on the London market, and cargoes which did not arrive in time for the auctions had to meet expensive storage charges. A ship which could be relied upon to catch the sales was assured of her cargoes. More than that, she could earn a bonus by taking the berth for last chance at the sales. Wool coming down late from the up-country stations in New South Wales could easily miss the January sales, and soon the *Cutty Sark* was promoted to the small band of super-clippers which undertook to leave her loading port late and arrive at her discharging port early. So there was business in employing

clippers in such a trade, and there still was real merit
—and profit—in racing. No wonder the *Cutty Sark*
came into her own at last.

In this she was immensely aided by the appoint-
ment of an outstanding captain, Captain Richard
Woodget. Moore took her the first two wool runs and
did very well. Woodget had her for the following ten
Australian voyages and did magnificently. Moore's
total pay from Willis for handling the little clipper
was only £200 a year. There was still a tradition
in those days that a ship-master could legitimately
add to his earnings by his own ventures, not by
robbing the ship and crew as a fool like Bruce did,
but by using his business sense (and a little space in
the ship) to his own profit. A sensible shipmaster,
accustomed to a certain trade, would soon have his
contacts at both ends, and would know the items
he could dispose of with advantage. He knew the
port authorities. Many captains carried business men
as passengers and made profitable contacts in that
way. A venture might be liquor, or millinery, or a
particular breed of dog—anything that would sell on
a sellers' market. Part of a captain's emoluments
had traditionally been the right to space in his ship
for his own ventures. At £200 a year it was necessary.
There were no pension schemes for shipmasters in
those days but, apart from the inherently indigent
(who did not often rise to command) and the hopelessly drunk (who never kept command if they got it)
not many shipmasters ended their days in the poor-
house. Most of them were able to retire ashore with

at least a competence, and set up a flagstaff in the garden of some pleasant country cottage.

A shipmaster who could earn something for himself was usually the best man for his owner, too. Woodget had shown his merit by making money handsomely for his owner in one of Willis's worst ships, the ancient *Coldstream,* and by getting better passages out of the old-timer than anyone else had been able to do throughout the previous thirty-five years of her undistinguished existence. He was the obvious choice for the *Cutty Sark.* He was that rarity, the right man in the right place at the right time. Richard Woodget ᴧwas a great shipmaster. He deserved the *Cutty Sark* and the *Cutty Sark* deserved him. I can think of no finer compliment to either.

His achievements with the grand little ship were the more meritorious since he had nothing in his favour. Willis had discovered long before that he could reduce the crew by a third, and he had promptly done so. Now, half the crew consisted not of competent grown seamen at all, but a group of boys. It was Willis's good fortune and in no way his merit —though it *was* Woodget's merit—that these boys generally showed themselves to be even better than men. Some of them were only twelve or thirteen years of age when they joined the clipper. Years afterwards one of the last of the sailing-ship owners was to keep a fleet going on the strong backs of boys, and to charge them for working for him, into the bargain. Old Willis had shown the way.

Another disadvantage Woodget had to face, and

that was the fact that each year it was becoming
more difficult for a small ship to pay on one Australian
round voyage, and yet there was no other work the
Cutty Sark could do. Her actual sailing time during
most of the ten years that Woodget had her was
rarely more than five months a year—about seventy
days out to Australia and around eighty days back.
(It was farther to sail coming back ; Cape Horn is
a long way south.) She could load all the general
cargo she was likely to get in a couple of weeks in
London, and screw a maximum capacity of wool
bales into her tight hull in Sydney or Newcastle in
considerably less than a month. This meant that
the ship was fully employed for little more than half
the year. Yet she had often to wait for her wool
cargo in Australia for months and months. Moreover, she had to be kept in full commission during
this wait and, because she was such a fine-lined ship,
she would not stand up without a good deal of ballast.
This ballast had to be bought, and people paid to
put it aboard, and then to take it out again and
dispose of it. Nobody gave sailing-ships anything.
Apprentices were cheap crew, but they had to be fed.
There were generally also six or eight able seamen,
and there was an afterguard to pay and feed as well.

There was no hope of earning anything by taking
a cargo of coal up to China or across to Chile while
she waited for the wool. That way she might miss
the wool, and she would get no return cargo from
either country. To romp up to Shanghai with the
trade winds was all very well, but it was a mighty

long way back again. A clipper like the *Cutty Sark* might run from Newcastle to Valparaiso in four weeks or less, but then she would have to discharge her own coal, pay for lightering, and then buy ballast expensively and wander back before the light Pacific trades. That might well take even a clipper fifty days. Nor could she carry coal enough to pay. As ships increased in size, freights had a habit of dropping. More and more had to be crammed into big square holds to hope to pay at all. The *Cutty Sark* could carry 1,200 tons of coal at the best. Ships carrying 3,000 tons, with a crew no larger than she had, were having trouble to make ends meet.

After all, there was one criterion by which the sailing-ship, clipper or whatever she might be, must stand or fall. She had to earn more than it cost to run her and, on top of that, she had to earn the cost of a ship to replace her during her useful sailing life, or her owner stood a good chance of going out of business. She had to earn enough to pay all her insurance premiums, and re-classification costs, and voyage expenses, and everything else. A ship was —and still is—fair game for port authorities everywhere. She was—and still is—a dreadfully expensive property, as soon as she could no longer earn enough to pay her way. It didn't matter in the least how beautiful she was or how astonishing her voyages were if they did not pay.

These problems were worrying old Willis, diehard that he was, more and more. They also worried Captain Woodget. He was a good owners' man, and he did his best to keep the ship's expenses down and give her a chance to pay. Those long waits in Sydney were pleasant, but they were expensive. Year by year the increasing horde of hungry steamers was creeping into all the ports of the world in endless quest of cargoes. The Sydneysiders cheered the little clipper for her wonderful runs, but the business-men could only afford to ship by her so long as a better means of getting their wool to England did not come along.

Meanwhile, voyage after voyage, Woodget drove the *Cutty Sark*, undermanned (by older standards) and cut-down, as she had never been driven before. He kept the ship in perfect trim and he sailed her perfectly, too. He was a seaman of skill and endless energy, and his nerve was as sound as his ship. A strict disciplinarian, he was a just man, and his officers, cadets, and able seamen respected and admired him. Gone were the days of foolish crew troubles, which had never been the fault of the ship. The men treated justly, responded, and they stayed in the ship year after year. Woodget drove the ship and he drove them, but he over-drove neither. He was one of those extraordinary men who was supremely good at whatever he undertook to do. He was a great navigator, an artist at sail-making, a master rigger. He bred collies, and his dogs were better than most other collies. He took up photography— in those days an almost impossible art to practise afloat—and he did excellently at that. He took a keen interest in his cadets though many of his fellow shipmasters felt under no obligation to do that, and he trained them—indeed, reared is a better word, for many of them came to him as children—so well that most of them made their mark in after-life, and many were outstanding.

The ship, while he was at Sydney waiting for the wool-clip to come down, was a happy abode of hard-working mariners in half-deck and forecastle. While the ship lay off in one of Sydney's lovely bays, with other clippers at anchor near her and the ferries passing by, the favourite dogwatch pastime was making music. The apprentices and the seamen would gather by the main hatch and sing their hearts out, some playing tunes—more or less correctly—with whatever came to hand, old whistle or comb with a bit of old paper on it, moistened in the mouth, or a jews' harp. The bursts of song coming over the lovely waters of the Sydney bays as clipper after clipper would take up the chorus, were a familiar feature of the sailing-ship life, as the crews, hard-worked and hard-muscled, slim and magnificently fit, rolled out their manly songs. Picnics in the ships' boats at week-ends, entertainments arranged by the hospitable Australians—who always took a great interest in the ships that were their link with " home "—evening concerts, and the day's hard work, made the time fly.

Again, it is a tribute to Woodget that none of his boys ever deserted, though desertions were common from sailing-ships then. Pay and prospects alike were better in Australia than they ever could be for

a Limejuice lad, bound 'prentice to a wool-clipper
or any other kind of sailing-ship. But the *Cutty
Sark* boys knew what they were doing. Their ships
were their public schooling, their indentures to life
as well as to the sea profession. It was their in-
estimable privilege to serve their time in a ship which
called to all the best in them, under a man who knew
how to bring that best out, and did. No wonder the
Cutty Sark lads under Woodget became commodores
in the P. & O.! The pity is that there were not
more of them ; that Willis, far-sighted as he was,
did not keep on the ship as a cadet-ship under Woodget
and man her with apprentices alone—twenty or thirty
of them—with a stiffening of petty officers.

The apprentices were not the only interesting
characters under Woodget in the *Cutty Sark*. Such
an unusual shipmaster gathered unusual men round
him, and even the cook was outstanding. The cook
was a Chinaman with the very English name of Tony
Robson. Many years before, a China clipper home-
ward bound came upon a small boat, drifting alone
in the China Sea. In the boat was a baby, and
nothing else. No food, no message, no anything.
The baby was well nourished and had not been long
adrift. Where did he come from ? What could
possibly be his story ? No one knew. No one ever
did know. The little Chinese baby was adopted by
the clipper crew and brought up to be a splendid
sailor. When Woodget had the *Cutty Sark*, this
Chinaman was an old man. He had graduated to
the galley, which was often a " soft " job for a good

old hand then. He was a first-class cook and a wonderful yarn-spinner, and though officially the cook, he still took a great interest in the rigging, and a fierce proprietary interest in the foremast which was nearest to his galley.

Out to New South Wales in seventy-five days, home again in under eighty—these were typical Woodget voyages. He did so well that old Willis, who never was a man to give up anything easily, had a last fling at breaking the China tea record. In 1886 he sent the *Cutty Sark* to Shanghai for a tea charter, for the last time. She had to take out a cargo of scrap-iron for nothing else was offering. This was a heavy, dead cargo which gave her poor chance of sailing. It was as well she earned the freight, however, for though she waited for months, no tea charter could be arranged. Willis had presented the ship with a golden shirt to fly at the main-truck before she set out on that voyage, but she was not to lower the *Thermopylae's* golden cock. The wonderful maiden voyage which that Aberdeen ship made—sixty days to Melbourne, twenty-eight days NSW to Shanghai, ninety-one days home with her tea—was to stand. Willis had to order Woodget to sail the *Cutty Sark*, golden shirt and all, down to Sydney in ballast to try to salvage something from the voyage, with a cargo of wool. In that trade she showed that she could defeat the wonderful *Thermopylae*, and she proceeded to do it.

At that time the ship that could outsail the *Thermopylae* could rate herself the fastest sailer in the

F

world.   The *Cutty Sark* put up records which stand
to-day at Lloyd's of London—sixty-seven, sixty-nine,
seventy days, Sydney or Newcastle to the Channel.
She was the *Queen Elizabeth* of the wool-clipper race,
and the *Thermopylae* was a splendid *Queen Mary*.
Under Woodget the *Cutty Sark* was indeed a queen
of the sea.

But it was all in vain.   Soon Willis knew it was
in vain.   So did Woodget.   None of the fine boys
who trained under him stayed in sailing-ships.   One
after the other they graduated into the despised
steamers to make their careers in powered vessels.
The almost incredible amount of effort that went
into the making of a clipper's Cape Horn voyage
made magnificent seamen, too.   But the clippers were
reduced to training seamen for their implacable rivals.
The men they made were forced to help to destroy
them.

Chapter Six

LAST OF A GLORIOUS ERA

A T the end of 1952 a few men still live who served in the *Cutty Sark* in her heyday in the Australian trade. One of these is Walter Naylor, who was second mate when the little ship beat the P. & O. mail steamer into Sydney, to the delight of the Australians who were carrying on a campaign for faster mail steamers at the time. They applauded the *Cutty Sark* vociferously, but they knew that her feat —though common enough for Woodget and her— was a rare gesture and really, a useless one, a sort of kick from a race-horse at an automobile. They continued to book passage to England in the automobile, and to send their fast freight by the same means. There was a hollow ring to the cheers, spontaneous as they were. The march of progress was not to be stayed by a beautiful ship. The day was almost over when men could afford to send their goods in an ocean-going yacht, or care to.

Another ancient mariner still on deck from those stirring days is Captain C. E. Irving, C.B., R.D., R.N.R. (retired). Born in 1871, Captain Irving went to sea at the age of twelve as an apprentice to John Willis in the ship *The Tweed*. At the age of thirteen he was transferred to the *Cutty Sark*, and in her

he sailed from 1885 to 1888, with Woodget—out to
China on the scrap-iron voyage, and in the wool
races round the Horn. Before he was seventeen the
youthful Irving had finished his indentures and presented himself for examination as second mate. But
the regulations were that candidates must have turned
seventeen, and he had to go back to sea again for a
Western Ocean voyage.

When he had his certificates he presented himself
for selection as an officer before the nabobs of the
P. & O. Company. The P. & O. was, in a way,
the successor of the mighty Honourable East India
Company, and it still kept up a great style. Officers
might not be paid very much—and they were not—
but they were expected at all times to present an
impeccable appearance and to behave like gentlemen.
Frock coats, and the complete set of formalities that
goes with that rig, were necessary even to pass the
front door. Irving must have looked very youthful
in this formal rig. The morning he presented himself there were dozens of other qualified officers,
senior to and older than himself, some of them from
the crack training-ships. The personnel director
looked him up and down.

" You're young, aren't you ? "

" Yes, sir," said Irving, meekly.

" What experience have you had ? "

" I served my time in the *Cutty Sark*, sir."

" What, under Woodget ? And you're still alive ? "

" Yes, sir. With Captain Woodget."

The director looked hard at him for a moment.

Cadets from the *Worcester* helped to bring the *Cutty Sark* back to London. Here they are stowing the jibs.

Arriving in London, with H.M.S. *Worcester* in the background.

Looking aft along the main deck.

Looking forward. The structure abaft the mainmast was added by H.M.S. *Worcester* to give access to the tweendecks.

Then he told him the firm of tailors which the company used. Irving was hired.

It required no greater skill or good fortune to survive in the *Cutty Sark* than in most other clippers in the Cape Horn trade, though she was known as a wet ship and Woodget was a hard driver. Shipowners were well aware that three or four years under such a man, in such a ship, was the best possible introduction to the seafaring world that a youngster could have. Trained in such a manner, a young man knew not only his business, but that it *was* his business. There was no doubt that seafaring would be his career. The P. & O. regarded their officers as an investment : a young man from Woodget's *Cutty Sark* was worth investing in.

They were right about Irving. He rose to command the greatest ships in the line, to distinguish himself by outstanding feats of seamanship again and again, to have a long and honourable career in the Merchant and Royal Navies alike. In command of the liner *Maloja* when she was sunk in the first World War, his conspicuous success in saving lives earned the thanks of the King, expressed personally. He must be one of the very few reserve officers—if not the only one—who became training commander of the Navy's gunnery school, H.M.S. *Excellent*, at Portsmouth. At 81, Captain Irving (having ferried small craft across the North Atlantic during the second World War because the Admiralty thought him rather old for active service) is still an active business man in London, with many shipping interests.

I talked with Captain Irving at the rooms of the Royal Empire Society, on Northumberland Avenue. Though it was then well over sixty years since he had left her, the *Cutty Sark* came booming through those London club-rooms under a stately cloud of sail, and the Cape Horn voice of the long-dead Woodget roared in a gale of wind, while Captain Irving yarned. What a life it was ! Irving was at the wheel once when Woodget did something rare for him. He drove the sticks out of her. The ship was partially dismasted.

Actually, she was not being over-driven. Any fool could over-drive a ship, and there were some notorious masters who retired to their cabins in a gale with a bottle or a case of bottles, and from the alcoholic " safety " of the poop breathed fire at any who wished to reduce sail. Woodget was not that kind of driver. Far from it ! He neither drank nor smoked, and he was a past-master at the art of keeping just that amount of sail on a ship which, with the winds blowing and the sea running, would allow her to do her maximum speed. His expertness and his daring alike consisted in keeping up that maximum speed. To overdo it was to invite trouble, and he knew that very well. This night it was a shift of wind that took the ship and whipped some of the lighter sticks out of her. It was a dreadful night, blowing and howling, but normal Roaring Forties stuff. Rain squall after rain squall overtook the running ship, and the huge seas threatened to knock her over in her stride. Woodget had a press of sail on her. Other ships would have been reduced to lower tops'ils (in part to ensure their captains' sleep), but he knew that she could stand her full suit. With that powerful counter old Willis had built into her, she needed driving, and she could stand it.

But a flick of the wind a few points of the compass momentarily took the sails aback. The whole wonderful engineering job of a clipper's rig was designed to take stresses from one side only, and that was abaft the sails. If the wind jumped round the sails—took them aback as sailors say, blew upon them from ahead—then the stouter stays helped to pull the masts down and not to support them. In the twinkling of an eye, the fore topmast and the main topgallant had come down on deck, and the masts and yards and thrashing sails were jumping and banging and clattering and smashing into the little ship's wooden sides, as if their only aim was to break her open, to bring her down in her stride. Still she ran on, for skilful handling brought her before the wind again. The sea was higher, the wind screaming. The little ship leapt and jumped and flung her long jib-boom now into the pressing dome of the rain-filled sky, now, as she slithered down the slope of an enormous sea, towards the very bowels of the earth. Seas crashed and thundered aboard her. The blown-out sails were making terrifying noises like a devil's bombardment, or the thunderclaps of doomsday.

The main topmast—a solid spar—and the topgallant-mast above it, and the fore topgallant and all the main tops'l and topgallant yards, and the fore

topgallant and the fore royal, were continuing their
attack upon the sides of the ship and along her rail
where they had fallen, as if the attack was under the
demoniac brain of a monster, and the ship shuddered
from the blows.   How could wooden sides stand
such hammering ? All hands were on deck, of course,
under the Herculean Woodget who was at his best
in such conditions.   They had to clear the mess,
save what they could, prevent the ship being stove
in by the smashing of her broken rigging.   They
had to work more in the sea than out of it, for at the
wheel where he was, Irving could not distinguish
where the sea ended, and the ship began.   If he had
not been lashed, he could not have stayed there.   The
sprays were picked up from the mighty combers and
flung at him like frozen needle-points, and the wind
tried to pick him up and blow him into the mizzen
rigging.   The long, long hours of the dreadful night
dragged by, and still the tremendous task went on.

Yet by the sullen daybreak of a morning young
Irving had expected not to see, the wreckage *had*
been cut away.   The ship *was* under full and competent
control again.   She raced on under the reduced sail
area forced upon her by the accident, and Woodget
began at once—*at once*—to re-rig her thoroughly, to
get another main topmast aloft and cross new yards
(for the clippers carried plenty of spare spars), and
drive along.   For two days the work went on, steadily,
despite the fact that even the wonderful Chinese cook
could not provide a warm meal, for the galley was
awash.   The half-deck was awash.   The poop was

awash. The forecastle was awash. There wasn't a dry place anywhere, except in the hold, and that was hermetically sealed.

When she was rigged again, the *Cutty Sark* ran on to Sydney, storming two thousand miles in a week, running often at seventeen knots, and averaging fifteen for days on end. Day after day, night after night, Captain Woodget stood on his poop, clinging with one hand to the weather mizzen rigging, or stamped the brief space between the binnacle and the rail. Standing under the wretched shelter of a minute weather-cloth lashed in the mizzen shrouds, a corner of his moustache gripped in his mouth to prevent it trailing off in the wind, his grey old beard glistening with salt and with rain—fearless, supremely competent, ready to react instantly to any emergency that might arise, and react with precise and immediate knowledge of the right thing to do—the brains of his ship. There stood Woodget, a magnificent representative of a great profession. There stood Woodget, voyage after voyage, year after year, getting the best out of his ship and all on board, driving for ever from her graceful decks the taint of the buckos and the few fools who once had blemished them.

Storming through the Roaring Forties, dodging the ice-islands and the floe-ice on the long and gale-ridden road towards Cape Horn, nursing her through doldrums calm and slogging her down-Channel into some wretched south-west gale, getting always the best out of that wonderful ship as no man had ever done before or would do again, Richard Woodget was indeed a Man amongst men, a Sailor with few peers anywhere, and no superiors at his chosen trade. Great ships made way for the *Cutty Sark*, and dipped their colours before her onrush. At last the *Thermopylae* was well beaten. The glorious *Mermerus*, the racing *Cimba*, the powerful *Rodney* and *Derwent*, the big, well-handed *Lochs*, the iron *Aristides*, *Salamis*, *Patriarch*, *Orontes*, *Thyatira*—a hundred lovely ships with a hundred lovely names, she raced and beat them all, year after year.

Yet it was not just a picture of a supreme deep-water sailorman I gathered, that afternoon in the rooms on Northumberland Avenue from my friend, Captain Irving. Woodget was an outstanding character in other ways. The *Cutty Sark* had—still has—splendid decked 'tween decks. When she was in ballast these were empty, and it was Woodget's joy to go roller-skating round them, and teach his officers and cadets to do likewise. He used to roller-skate on the main-deck too, but that was full of houses, hatches, masts, fife-rails, and the like. In the 'tween-decks there was only the chance of pitching into the lower hold. On the main-deck, you could go overboard. As a change from roller-skating, Woodget took up cycling, on the ballast run to Sydney from China, and he taught himself to be an expert cyclist in those same 'tween decks. That was dangerous, for the hatches were all open, and a pitch of the ship could easily send him helplessly down. His dog-watch amusement in the good weather of that run was to teach the apprentice to cycle, too, and some of them did not take kindly to it. His cycle was one of the early two-wheelers, a bone-shaker by name and a bone-shaker in fact. The pedals were on the high front wheel, and it lacked springs and all other refinements.

Woodget took up nothing he was not thorough with. The bane of young Irving's life was, when recovering from bone-shaker saddle sores or a bump on the skull caused by roller-skating on a rolling deck, to be chosen as one of the crews of the two lifeboats old Woodget used to put out, lashed together with a plank across to support the tripod for his ancient camera, while he egged them on and somehow achieved the apparently impossible feat of getting a " shot " of the ship under sail while the camera was properly steady, a thousand miles and more from the nearest land.

What a man to sail with !

Yet by the mid-nineties it was impossible for the *Cutty Sark* to pay her way. The wool-clippers were bigger and bigger, and the wool ship race was dying anyway. The steamers by then had the lions' share of the general cargoes and the wool in the Australian trade, and the little clipper could not hope to pay on less expensive cargoes. No one cared if she raced home in sixty days with 1,200 tons of grain. Indeed, the brokers might well be annoyed, for she would give their cargo too brief a warehousing. Big sailers soon were getting grain because they could be trusted to deliver it slowly, not quickly. The day of the sleek and lovely little clipper yacht was over. Small cargoes carried expensively could never hope to pay again, and she had to go.

By 1895 such giant sailing-ships as the five-masters *France* and *Potosi*, carrying well over six times the cargo the *Cutty Sark* could, and with less than twice her crew, were already in the water. The *Thermopylae* had been sold to Canada for five years and was still smashing records in the trans-Pacific trade. The two magnificent ships still were fighting hard.

They had played their glorious part in maintaining the greatness of the British merchant service. Their day was really done—had been well on the way out, indeed, when they were launched. It was their own magnificence that had kept them going for so long, for they were better ships even than their owners, their designers, and their builders had dreamed of.

·In the end both were sold to those good judges of good ships, the Portuguese. The *Thermopylae* became the training-ship *Pedro Nunez* for the Portuguese Navy, and the *Cutty Sark* became the trader *Ferreira* belonging to some brothers of that name in Lisbon. They were able to use her successfully for almost the next quarter of a century. She was a strong ship and her hull continued in splendid condition. So long as she had a rag to show to the wind she could sail. Again she was battered by hurricanes and alarming gales. Again she had her rudder torn away by the sea and sailed hundreds of miles with a makeshift rigged by her Portuguese master. She took the ground in a

The *Cutty Sark* was moored close by the *Worcester*, off Greenhithe.

The old clipper survived the war. But her rigging deteriorated.

The yacht-like hull is still seen to perfection.

The *Cutty Sark* in January, 1953.

West Indies hurricane and was given up as a total
constructive loss by the pessimists ashore. But she
came off as good as ever and continued in her Atlantic
round—Lisbon or Oporto, New Orleans, Rio, the
Portuguese possessions of the West African coast,
the Cape Verde Islands.

Seriously dismasted, she was re-rigged as a barquentine. Still she sailed splendidly whenever she
had a chance. Still that noble hull, which was so
light and graceful it looked as if a child's hand would
give it way with a push from alongside a dock wall,
moved wonderfully through the water whenever the
wind blew. She sailed unscathed through the '14–'18
War, except for the damage that hurricanes did her.
Now and again she showed herself briefly in famous
ports—Liverpool, Cardiff, London—though for the
most part her life lay at open roadsteads where lowly
ships, under-capitalised and run with a minimum of
outgoings, might hope to pick up slow cargoes and
somehow make ends meet. The Portuguese did their
best to keep her employed, but it was difficult. I
have spoken to some of them who were in the ship
during these years, and their admiration for her
is still profound—profound, and based on under-
standing.

By 1922 the *Cutty Sark* was no longer able to earn
her living anywhere. Too small for long trades, too
big and too deep for short, too finely lined to drift
with a dullard's load of hides or guano along America's
west coast—that last home of so many square-rigged
ships—she was caught, too, in the post-war shipping

depression. There was no hope for her. In these circumstances a public-spirited British shipmaster came upon her, driven by stress of weather into Falmouth. He could scarcely believe his eyes. The *Cutty Sark* still afloat? That noble model of the sailing art, that triumph of the adze and the rigging loft! The strange name and the strange flag, the barquentine rig, the line of painted ports along her sides like the old East Indiamen, could not disguise her. Captain Dowman had once been passed at sea by the *Cutty Sark* in the great days when Woodget had her. Once seen, never forgotten! Now he found that he could buy the great old ship, and preserve her. First she had to complete her voyage, and then he had her towed back to Falmouth from the Portuguese coast.

It was a great gesture, worthy of the ship and of the best of shipmasters. Captain Dowman restored the clipper to her proper status, and made use of her as best he could, as a training-ship for boys. It was his desire to give her a full suit of sails again and send her off to sea. But he died before this had been done. His widow presented the ship to the Thames Nautical Training College, and in 1938, with Captain Woodget aboard once more from his well-earned retirement, the *Cutty Sark* was towed round to the Thames. She was moored close to the training-ship *Worcester*. There she remained, doing splendid work, throughout the second World War, with the bombers flying over her and, far too often in the war's early years, high-explosive and fire bombs falling close. But she survived.

There she remained until the *Cutty Sark* Preservation Society was formed to take her over in 1952, with the purpose of preserving her as the National Monument the great and graceful little ship most surely is. The last of a glorious era, indeed she is, and one of the noblest of them all.

The others have all gone. The *Thermopylae* and the *Thomas Stephens* were sunk outside the Tagus when their working lives were over, though their great rival had then twenty years of hard tramping still ahead of her, and two World Wars. The lovely old *Samuel Plimsoll* was a coal-hulk in Fremantle for many years, and finally went down there at her berth. Few other real clippers saw even the nineteenth century out, though an odd one dragged on a few years in the Indian Ocean. By the mid-nineteen-fifties all the big cargo-carrying sailing-ships were gone, too—*all* engineless commercial square-rigged ships, gone from the face of the sea, wiped away like the morning mist. Here and there a ship has been saved and preserved as a museum-piece, to show future generations what such vessels looked like— the frigate *Constitution* at the Boston Navy Yard ; the frigate *Jylland* in Copenhagen ; the ships *C. W. Morgan* and *Joseph Conrad* at Mystic, in Connecticut ; the ship *Af Chapman* at Stockholm ; the four-masted *Pommern* at Mariehamn and the *Viking* at Gothenburg ; the little barque *Seute Deern* at Hamburg, where in 1952 she was a restaurant. A few odd old-timers still showed a yard or two at odd corners of the globe, and there was still a considerable fleet of square-rigged school-ships, carrying no cargoes and engaged entirely upon short voyages designed for training boys.

Of all these ships—of *all* ships—only the *Cutty Sark* now survives intact as a relic of the wonderful clippers, a worthy example of the great pioneering days of Sail.